# This Feels Like Home

"Whether your life is seemingly problem free or beset by challenges, loneliness, doubts, or heartache, Autumn invites you to find hope, peace, encouragement, refreshment, and meaning. With honesty and transparency, Autumn's words speak to the heart as she leads all into the arms of Jesus, the ultimate burden-bearer, need-meeter, soul-uplifter, redeemer."

**—SHARON SHEARMAN,** Director of Family Ministry, St. Paul's Lutheran Church, Des Peres, MO

"In a world where so many people feel like they have no friends, Autumn invites 'her friends' and others like them to consider how friendship with God could be life changing. This uplifting collection of real-life struggles and joys connects us to the deeper meaning and sustainable sources of support in the gospel. Read it each morning with your cup of coffee or stretch out in a hammock and soak in these reflections for your soul."

**—HUGH BARLETT,** Senior Pastor, Chesterfield Presbyterian Church, Chesterfield, MO

"Having known Autumn for almost 20 years, I can confidently say her new book is true-Autumn—where she has been and where she hopes more of us can explore with her. She takes us to a place where love rules—rather than fear. A place in our hearts and actions that is so freeing—as she says, 'Hey sis, you are significant, but you aren't sovereign.' I devoured this book, which showed me that Autumn knew I needed to drink these words and renew my spirit. Read, feel, and know you are not alone."

**—PENNY PENNINGTON**, St. Louis, MO

AUTUMN E. SCHOECK

# This Feels Like Home

Inspirations for Finding Peace

RIVER GROVE
BOOKS

Published by River Grove Books
Austin, TX
www.rivergrovebooks.com

Distributed by River Grove Books

Design and composition by Greenleaf Book Group
Cover design by Greenleaf Book Group
Cover illustration copyright © 2025 by Gigi DeMaggio

Publisher's Cataloging-in-Publication data is available.

Print ISBN: 978-1-63299-958-0

eBook ISBN: 978-1-63299-959-7

First Edition

For Andy, who always thought I could.
(And even if he didn't, he never said a word.)

# Contents

Foreword | xiii

Preface | xv

Author's Note | xix

Introduction | 1

**WHEN YOU HOLD THE KEYS TO HOME**

I Want to Go Home | 7

Who's Invited? Everyone. | 10

Even There | 12

Attention! Good People Do Not Go to Heaven! | 14

It's a Relationship, Not a Religion | 17

**WHEN YOU SEE THE ADORING
EYES OF YOUR FATHER**

Remember Who You Are and Whose You Are | 23

Jesus Looked at Him and Loved Him | 26

Today You Will Be with Me in Paradise | 29

Filled with Compassion | 32

There Are No Orphans | 35

Texting with Jesus | 38

## WHEN YOU UNDERSTAND WHO HE IS AND WHO YOU ARE NOT

To Understand, We Must First Rewind | 43

I Am Peter | 46

You Are Significant, but Not Sovereign | 49

Even Dolly Falls Short | 52

Solitude | 55

Rich in Spirit | 58

## WHEN YOU THINK YOU'RE NOT ENOUGH

Fear Is a Liar | 63

He Made You That Way for a Reason | 66

That Gray Is a Crown of Splendor | 69

A Time for Every Season under Heaven | 72

You're Going the Wrong Way | 74

You Are a Work in Progress | 77

He Will Never Stop Pursuing You | 79

## WHEN YOU SAY, "TELL ME MORE ABOUT JESUS"

The Alabaster Flask | 85

Prayer Unlocks the Doors of Heaven | 88

He Doesn't Deserve This | 91

What's Good for the Goose
Is Good for the Gander(s) | 94

Every Step, Jesus Is There | 97

God Answers All Prayers | 99

Yours Is the Kingdom of Heaven | 102

**WHEN YOUR STRUGGLE BECOMES REAL**

Can We Be Real for Just a Minute? | 107

The Lord Is Turning Toward You | 111

May Your Bible Be Tattered | 114

Alone | 117

When God Is All You Have,
You Realize God Is All You Need | 120

Your Faith Has Healed You | 123

**WHEN WORRY AND WAITING WEIGH ON YOU**

Cancel Out the Noise | 129

If You Fail to Plan | 132

Could We Achieve Contentment? | 135

The Invasive Weeds | 138

You Can See It Like This. Or That. | 141

Consider the Source of Those Thoughts | 145

Forty | 147

Jesus Can Take You from Gloom to Bloom | 150

## WHEN YOU ARE WEAK AND HE IS STRONG

To Know Him Is to Love Him | 155

What a Friend We Have in Jesus | 158

Because God Is Good | 161

O Come Let Us Adore Him | 163

It Is Not You Speaking | 166

Eye on the Prize | 169

For Thine Is the Kingdom | 171

## WHEN YOU LOVE YOUR NEIGHBOR

Don't Judge a Person by Their . . . | 175

You Say It Best When You Say Nothing at All | 178

Seventy-seven Times | 181

Walking Pace | 184

Love One Another | 186

Intercede | 189

CONTENTS

## WHEN YOU SURRENDER AND GO

It's Not about You | 195

Follow Me | 198

This, Then, Is How You Pray | 200

Go | 202

Let Down Your Nets | 204

The Laws of Love | 207

All for His Glory | 210

Go—Tell Your Story | 213


Acknowledgments | 217

About the Author | 221

# *Foreword*

I f I'm being honest, the idea of writing the foreword for
a devotional is very intimidating. What could I possibly
say to inspire someone to keep turning the page? The
truth is that I love Jesus and am a follower of His Word.
My favorite (and only memorized) Bible verse is "Love
one another as I have loved you" (John 13:34). But my
knowledge of biblical facts certainly does not run as deep
as the Red Sea.

However, I do know *some* things. I know what it means
to be flawed and still loved, to sin and to be forgiven. I know
what it means to be brought to your knees in worry and to
rejoice. I know what it is like to have fear and worry con-
sume you to the point that you feel utterly paralyzed and
powerless. In those moments, like many of us, I turn to my
best friend. And in those moments—whether it be through
miles and miles of walks, front porch visits, or sunning on
the deck before school pickup—my friend, Autumn, has

always reminded me to turn it over to Jesus. Not in a Holy Roller way. Not in a preachy way. But in a humble and *human* way. In a way that is perfectly, uniquely Autumn. The way that makes you feel like you can exhale and let go. So when she told me she wanted to write a devotional, I knew there would be no one better to share Jesus's message in a relatable way.

For more than a decade, I've been lucky enough to call Autumn my friend. In that time, I have grown in my relationship with God. I have seen how I am uniquely and perfectly loved by Him. I have given Him my deepest fears and thanked Him for the biggest blessings. I have learned that it isn't the depth of my knowledge that He wants, but rather my constant love and complete surrender. I hope that by turning the page, you will also come to know how loved you are by Him. Now, go and see what comes next.

—Julie Cooper,
St. Louis, Missouri

# Preface

Midlife.

It's where I currently find myself and where I am, surprisingly, settling in quite well. There is something about this stage of life that has colored me *tired*, but not in the sense you might imagine. Heck yes, I am *physically* tired, but I am mostly tired of dreaming and not doing, fearing and not trusting, and talking but not walking. I have encouraged so many to walk in faith, lean on Jesus, and trust the next step—yet *I* have hesitated.

Since I was little, I knew I had a story to tell. I have started and stopped writing many "books" over the years, abandoning ship when my doubts consumed me. But it's time. So here I sit—scared, but ready.

How often do we feel that in life? *Scared, but ready.*

For me, I have been scared more than I have ever been ready. Fear has not been a friend of mine. It has actually been the biggest hindrance in my life. But those fears, although great in number, have led me into the arms of the most loving man I know: Jesus.

My anxieties, fears, and worries have been, dare I say, blessings in my life. I have come to see this now, and I so desperately want others to see that when they are weak, He (Jesus) is strong.

Friend, you don't have to carry all of it. Whatever "it" is for you, there is Someone who wants to walk that road with you. I have walked the road of desperation, loneliness, and worry; the only place I have ever found true peace is in the arms of Jesus. I'm not sure how to explain it, but this book is my attempt.

Frederick Buechner once said, "The place God calls you to is the place where your deep gladness and the world's deep hunger meet." I love that so much. My deepest gladness is talking about Jesus. The world's deepest hunger seems to be the need for Jesus. A match made in Heaven. Literally.

Every morning for the last year, I wake up, put on my glasses, and head downstairs in wrinkled PJs and messed-up hair. With coffee in hand, I sit in my chair, a basket full of Bibles to my right, and lean into the only Truth I know. It's my scaffolding for the day, the structure I need in order for everything else to fall in line. It's where I talk to God, write about God, and pray that Jesus will open my eyes to His plan for me. It's where I feel most . . . at *home*.

It turns out that I absolutely have a story to tell. We all do—*His* story. In the words of the Casting Crowns, "I'm just a nobody, trying to tell everybody, all about Somebody who saved my soul."

Indeed.

I hope this book deepens your trust and love in the Creator of the universe; the Creator of the one and only *you*.

Love,
Autumn

# Author's Note

About a year ago I knew I wanted to spread the love of God to anyone who would listen, so I created a profile on Instagram (@autumn_schoeck). Many of these devotions originated from those writings.

I would love to hear your story. Please email me at autumn@autumnschoeck.com.

# Introduction

am not a theologian. Not even close. I am just a super-intense "feeler" who loves Jesus and wants everybody to know and feel His love for them. Those are my credentials. I hope they prove to be as useful as I believe them to be.

I wanted this book to read like you and I are sitting at a coffee shop, hands wrapped around a warm latte, hearts open, speaking the truth in love to one another. Those conversations are my favorite. Just like the words that my dearest friends and I have shared over the years, I want this to feel authentic and heartfelt. More than anything, I want it to land in the hands of *anyone* who needs it.

In the forefront of my mind, while I took "pen to paper," were several influential individuals. As I wrote, my words were directed toward each of them: the one who doesn't believe that he is good enough for Christianity, the one who believes that her "sin" is so big that there is no way she is still wanted by Jesus, and the one who never thought she had the "fancy words" to pray out loud or contribute to a Bible study.

For them, I write. For them, the Kingdom of Heaven awaits.

With this in mind, you will often find me explaining (and overexplaining because, well, that's what I do) the foundational concepts of Christianity, along with the most recited stories from the Bible. There are two reasons for that. First, I never want to assume that the person who is reading this book has been to church, to a Bible study, or even picked up a Bible. I am speaking here to the woman who just needs Jesus and isn't sure where to start. It's a "come as you are" kind of gathering, my friend. Second, the Word of God never tires or fails, so repeating what is already known is our way of speaking life into a dark world. Frankly, I don't think we could ever repeat it enough.

If this is your first brush with Christianity or devotionals, welcome. I am so glad you're here. And, I'm not sure how you feel about a daily devotional, but those have always felt a bit obligatory for me, leaving me to feel like I am behind or falling short if I forget a day . . . or two. I want this book to make you feel good, not defeated, so each devotion is just a story—a story that you can read at your own pace and in any order you wish. No pressure, no obligations, just an opportunity for you to experience the love of Jesus whenever you need it. Skip around, read it back-to-front, or dog-ear the corners of your favorite story; just know it's here when you need it.

Finally, you will always find two things in every devotion—a reference verse straight out of God's Word and a closing prayer. The prayer will always begin with "my Father," and my prayer for you is that you come to know Him as the personal, loving, nurturing Father that He is.

When You
Hold the Keys
to Home

# I Want to Go Home

But our citizenship is in Heaven, and from it we
await a savior, the Lord Jesus Christ . . .

**PHILIPPIANS 3:20**

live in a household of introverts, so hearing the phrase "I want to go home" is not unusual. It is, on the contrary, quite routine and even expected at most social outings we attend. Even I typically want to go home way earlier than most on any given Friday or Saturday night that we spend with friends.

Home.

Whether you grew up in a house filled with compassion or calamity, home is a place where we all *long* to go. If you grew up in the home resembling *Leave It to Beaver*, then you had a reason to long for home, and upon arrival your heart was at ease. If you grew up in a home where walking through the front door landed you on an emotionally unsteady and unpredictable ground, then you certainly longed for a place where you *could* feel peace and restoration. Either way, home is a place where we all *long* to be. We all want to go "home."

My daughter illustrated this perfectly as a young girl when she would enter our home still repeating, "I just want to go home." She would be so overly exhausted that even arriving at her home base still did not render her restored. Home for her was a state of mind, it was a place where she felt fully renewed—where she felt at *peace*. Even a young child, yet to encounter all the troubles of this world, still has a need to be renewed, which suggests that the longing for home defies the boundaries of age. From the moment we are born, we long for something this world cannot offer.

My sweet friend, we all long for the same thing. We all long for a place where we feel safe, protected, content, peaceful, and *loved*. That place, that Home, exists for all of us. And longing for it does not mean that you are ungrateful, depressed, or wanting to call it quits. It means that you were created for *more*, and to long for it reinforces that notion altogether.

The "more" for which you look will one day come. On that day, you will see the face of Jesus and be filled in a way of which only He is capable. It will feel like you have walked into a cozy, warm house with an apple pie baking in the oven and the very One who loves you most will stand before you, exclaiming, "My dear child, I am so glad you are Home. Sit. Rest."

*My Father, I long for the day when I can feel like all my needs are met at Home with You. I know this world is not my home, which makes each day seem difficult. Give me the strength to see this day through, understanding that You can meet all my needs if I just hand them over to You. Thank you for loving me and being my Father.*

*Amen.*

# Who's Invited? Everyone.

In my Father's house are many rooms. If it were not
so, would I have told you that I go to prepare a
place for you? And if I go and prepare a place
for you, I will come again and will take you to
myself, that where I am you may be also. And you
know the way to where I am going.

**JOHN 14:2–4**

New Year's Eve—a night that means going to bed
early for some and for others, staying up until the
wee hours. While one is attending a party or two,
another might be suffering from FOMO (fear of missing out) due to the absence of a party invite. I often have
JOMO (joy of missing out), always welcoming a quiet night
at home. Regardless of an invite or not, the day comes and
goes like any other and the clock turns forward at midnight.

But friend, listen up—there is a party, an unbelievable gathering, to which *you* are invited. Who else is invited, you might ask? Anyone. And everyone who desires to attend. It's the most inclusive party there is and ever will be.

An all-inclusive party might suggest it is basic, common, and lacks importance. On the contrary, this party brings joy, forgiveness, freedom, redemption, and eternal life. Now, you tell me: Who would not want to be on that guest list?!

As the verse states, there is plenty of room in the house of the Lord; no shortage of space. And just remember, no matter who you are or what you have done, you have an open invitation in hand. Whether or not you accept that invitation is up to you. He is a God who says "yes!" We are a people who often reply with "no." Let's see if we can change that with the turn of the clock. Here's to surrendering all to Jesus and loving like Him. Tell the others about the good news—that they, too, are invited.

*My Father, You are the Host of all Hosts. Thank you for inviting every single one of us to Your table. For those who feel lost, remind them they are known and loved. Lord, let us all be reminded today that we are part of Your family and that alone is enough.*

*Amen.*

# Even There

Even there your hand shall lead me,
and your right hand shall hold me.

**PSALM 139:10**

The words of Psalm 139 bring such comfort. I have started to read them weekly for this reason. The first verse, "Oh Lord, you have searched me and you know me," brings tears to my eyes. It strips me of all pride and brings me to a place of absolute humility; right at the feet of Jesus. How, oh how, does the Lord of the Universe know little ol' me? Because everywhere I go, He is there.

Even *there* (insert wherever *there* is to you), you might ask? Yes, even *there*.

I know that the Bible can feel a bit daunting. Where does one start?! The Old Testament can seem heavy, although it sets the stage perfectly for what's to come. The Gospels are great—lots of good news from Jesus there. Most quiet mornings, I end up reading the Psalms. David, the author of most Psalms, was just like us. He was full of sin, but chosen by God. Friend, you too are chosen. Let these precious prayers remind you of that.

You will see the utter humanity of David as he flips from woe to worship throughout every page. I don't know about you, but that sounds like a typical day for me! My entire life is full of vacillations from "Lord, help" to "Lord, thank you." And guess what: that's just where Jesus wants us, always relying on Him.

Since what I have written for today is brief, take a minute to read all of Psalm 139. Let those words permeate your entire being. Be reminded of the closeness of your Father. Even there, friend, His hand will guide you. Even there.

*My Father, thank you for Your most perfect*
*Words. Help us to find solace and comfort*
*when we lean into Your Word. When we*
*are in doubt, lead us to You always.*

*Amen.*

# Attention! Good People Do Not Go to Heaven!

For by grace you have been saved
through faith. And this is not your own doing;
it is the gift of God, not a result of works,
so that no one may boast.

**EPHESIANS 2:8–9**

Have you ever heard someone described as a "good Christian" or a "bad Christian"? Or even worse, "and to think they call themselves a Christian" (with an eye roll). Shoot, maybe it's even you who has uttered those words (no judgment). Either way, what kind of emotion do those phrases elicit in you? Let me ask it like this: How do those statements, maybe to those who have not yet come to know Jesus, make others *feel* about their chances of being accepted by Him?

Friends, we have got to clear something up for the man Himself. The reputation that He and *we* have been given is just not correct and it is not Christian. This whole notion of Christians being perfect and/or elitists who are free from all trouble and sin is wrong.

*Being good or bad does not have anything to do with getting into Heaven.*

Please read that again.

Heaven is full of "bad" Christians. I, Autumn, am a "bad" Christian. In fact, the only "good" Christian I know is the One at the very root of it all—Jesus. We all fall short of the glory of God. Every. Single. One. Of. Us.

Yes, absolutely you should strive to keep the commandments and live in a way that aligns with God's will. No question on that. Your ticket in, however, is not based on your behavior. I hope that brings immediate relief to you rather than fear. You can do as many acts of service as you can fit into one day, serve on a dozen church committees, pray out loud on every street corner in town, and lead every Bible study possible. Those will *still* not get you into Heaven.

Don't lose heart. This might seem contradictory to what you have been told and believe. But friend, good people do not go to Heaven—*believers go to Heaven.*

You can stop spinning your wheels measuring your worth and your success on earthly things. Jesus wants your heart and your trust in Who He is and what He has done. He has sacrificed His life for yours. He took on all of your "bad" Christian tendencies and took them right to the cross. He died for them and because of that, you don't have to lead or even participate in every Bible study in town (thank you, Jesus!).

It's called grace. You are saved by grace *alone*. Not because of what you have done, but because of what He has done. It is truly that simple. All you have to do is believe.

*My Father, I am a sinner in need of a Savior.*
*Thank you for taking on all of my bad habits,*
*behaviors, and tendencies so I can spend eternity*
*with You. I am undeserving and imperfect, but*
*yet You want me. How can it be? I know I cannot*
*earn eternity with You, so help me to receive You*
*and believe everything You have told me. In doing*
*this, I know that I will soon see You face to face.*

*Amen.*

# It's a Relationship, Not a Religion

And when Jesus heard it, he said to them,
"Those who are well have no need of a physician,
but those who are sick. I came not to call
the righteous, but sinners."

**MARK 2:17**

was raised in the Lutheran faith. I attended Holy Cross Lutheran School, where I learned the Nicene Creed, the Apostles' Creed, and memorized all the books of the Bible in order. In eighth grade I prepared for my confirmation and studied to pass my verbal and written tests. It was all part of the process. It was all part of the *religion*.

Before anyone thinks I am ganging up on the Lutherans, stay with me. I am still and will forever be a Lutheran—I am proud of my roots and the time I put into learning the fundamentals of the faith. For some, the rote memorization and man-made rules of religion are a hindrance that prevent them from leaning into Jesus. And that's just no good. That's not what Jesus wants.

Jesus just wants *you*.

Jesus is after one thing: your heart. He is motivated by His love for you, so before getting caught up in the rules that man has made, get caught up in the love Jesus has for you.

If you are hesitant, that's okay. But let me ask you this: *Why?* What is the risk of leaning into the love of Jesus? What do you have to lose? Truly. Remember our earlier devotion about thoughts the enemy puts in our minds. Thoughts that you are not good enough or forgiven or worthy of a Savior. Those thoughts are not from Jesus. Rather, they are keeping you *from* Him. Let's look at our verse for today—

"It is not the healthy who need a doctor, but the sick. I have not come to call the righteous, but the sinners" (Mark 2:17). This is one of my favorite verses in the Bible because it reminds us that Jesus always picked those who were the least deserving. He had no interest in the "perfect" or the "righteous." He wanted those who needed Him. And friend, we *all* need Him.

My guess is that every strong relationship in your life points back to one thing: love. Jesus *is* love. More than rote memorization, more than creeds, more than kneeling, standing, or sitting, He wants you to know Him. He wants a relationship with you. A relationship with Someone you cannot *see* is difficult, I realize. But He gets that and if you just ask, He will foster a connection in a way that you never could have imagined.

> *My Father, thank you for wanting me. Thank you for pursuing me and loving me. Help me to walk with You and realize that the schemes of the enemy are the only thing standing between You and me. Today I accept your invitation for a relationship with You.*
>
> *Amen.*

When You See
the Adoring Eyes
of Your Father

# Remember *Who You Are* and *Whose You Are*

But now thus says the Lord, he who created you,
O Jacob, he who formed you, O Israel:
"Fear not, for I have redeemed you;
I have called you by name, you are mine . . ."

**ISAIAH 43:1**

To whom do you belong?

That's quite a question, isn't it. If we polled a whole room of people, I am sure the answers would be all across the board. You might hear—

I belong to nobody.

I belong to myself.

I belong to the world.

I belong to my spouse, my parents, my dog, et cetera.

The potential answers are endless. When you are a follower of Christ, however, things take on a different look and feel. There seems to be only one answer to the question.

You belong to God. To Him you belong. You are His. You, my friend, are His beloved child. Don't let that scare or overwhelm you. Let me tell you why that is a good thing; a great thing.

When you are a child of God, you are who He says you are. He reminds us that He has called us each by name and we are His. What does being His mean? It means you are forgiven, redeemed, chosen, beloved, and more. I don't know about you, but that all sounds pretty amazing.

Do you have anyone in your life who feels that way about you? All the time?

Jesus does.

How amazing is it that the Creator of the universe, the King of Kings, has chosen you, called you by name, and considers you beloved? Let that sink in. You. Are. Beloved. No matter who you are or what you have done.

So next time you forget who you are or to whom you belong, let this be your reminder. He has called you by name and you are His. That is the finest blessing that you will ever receive.

*My Father, I am Yours. Thank you. You have chosen me and I am humbled by Your infinite grace and mercy. Jesus, fill me with Your Spirit on this day and help me to see that my purpose is found in You.*

*Amen.*

# Jesus Looked at Him and Loved Him

And Jesus, looking at him, loved him, and said to him, "You lack one thing: go, sell all that you have and give to the poor, and you will have treasure in Heaven; and come, follow me."

**MARK 10:21**

My favorite stories to read about Jesus are when He is loving the unlovable—which, let's be real, is pretty much always. That's just His thing, which is reason number 5,767 why He is the absolute best!

In Mark 10, we find Jesus talking to a man who had run up to Him, asking what he needed to do to inherit eternal life. This was a wealthy man, one who was quick to tell Jesus that he had kept all of the commandments. We can't fault the guy for believing that he had done everything to inherit the Kingdom of Heaven by keeping *all* of them.

We know, however, that keeping all of the commandments is impossible. Unless your name rhymes with Cheesus.

But being the patient, loving, gracious Father He is, instead of rolling His eyes and walking away, He looked at the man and *loved* him. See that? This undeserving man was given a look of endearment by Jesus, who could not help but to love him.

This man ended up refusing Jesus's request to give up all of his money to the poor and follow Him. Wowza, right? As you read that, are you tempted to reach into your pocket and grab a proverbial stone to throw? Are you ready to cast judgment on this selfish man? I'll admit, the guy sounds like a real dummy. But wait, hold on to your stone for a minute.

When we stop and ponder this story, what we find is yet another person who was not willing to put Jesus first. Would you agree? Now it's feeling a little harder for me to cast judgment, because what I see in this man is . . . *me*.

So let me ask you: do you always put Jesus first? If you're like me, it's my intention, but I repeatedly fall short. All of us have earthly desires that we often place ahead of Jesus. Maybe it's money, an addiction, a relationship, or even worry. No matter what it is, we are all that rich guy struggling to break free from the earthly chains that bind us. And we are *all* in chains, friends. Some of our chains are just harder to see.

There is only one way to break free and that is with the very man who created you. Where you can't, He can. If you think your chains are too heavy, pray. Ask Him to help you. Jesus looks at you and *loves* you, even when you don't deserve it.

*My Father, You are the God of all compassion and grace. No one is above You; only You have all that we need. Help us to give up ourselves and our earthly possessions for You. Help us to put You first always.*

*Amen.*

# Today You Will Be with Me in Paradise

Then he said, "Jesus, remember me when you come into your kingdom." Jesus answered him, "Truly, I tell you, today you will be with me in paradise."

**LUKE 23:42–43**

For those of you who have lost a loved one, I highly doubt you would ever describe that day as "good." In fact, it might be one of the saddest days of your life. So how on earth could a day filled with brutality, crucifixion, and death be labeled as "Good Friday"? Whether you are reading this on Good Friday or just any old Friday, the message is not to be missed.

We have to dig a little deeper and look beyond the physical realm that we typically revisit during Holy Week.

A revisiting is most definitely warranted, as it reminds us of the sacrifice that was made on our behalf. But again, *why* is this considered a *good* day?

Friend, this day is good because it points to our salvation. It is our day of hope and deliverance; the day when the sins of the world, including yours and mine, were taken away by Jesus Christ of Nazareth.

Jesus said very little as He endured terrible pain on this day. He was, after all, man in the flesh. His injuries hurt him just like they would physically hurt you and me. There was no time or energy for talking. What He did say, however, was full of hope. And it all happened in his final moments, as He hung on the cross to die.

The criminals, one to His left and one to His right, were hearing and watching it all. They heard Jesus say, "Father, forgive them, for they do not know what they are doing" (Luke 23:34). Sis, what Jesus said that day, about those criminals, He also says on our behalf at every moment. He says, "Father, forgive them." Sadly, we most often *do* know what we have done, yet we still do it—and He still forgives.

The most poignant moment on Good Friday, for me, happened after the criminals heard what Jesus had just said to the Father on their behalf. Now realizing that this man was the Messiah, one criminal asked Jesus to "remember him when He gets to His Kingdom . . ." And how did Jesus respond?

Jesus answered this man by saying, "Truly, I tell you, today you will be with me in paradise." It was a *yes*. Yes, my child, I *will* remember you.

This, friend, is Who your Savior is. He is forgiving right up until your final breath and is always making room for you at His table. Scooch over, buddy, make a seat for my other kiddo, says Jesus. Forever forgiving, forever loving, forever yours—if you just believe.

*My Father, You are eternally gracious and inclusive.*
*Thank you for receiving us into Your Kingdom.*
*Thank you for wanting us there with You, at the*
*table. When we forget who You are, remind us that*
*You are truly ours and that we are truly Yours.*

*Amen.*

# *Filled with Compassion*

Moved with pity, he stretched out his hand
and touched him and said to him, "I will; be clean."
And immediately the leprosy left him,
and he was made clean.

**MARK 1:41–42**

Think back to the year 2020. What comes to mind? Let me jog your memory—Dr. Fauci, social distancing, N-95 masks. COVID-19. The year 2020 was a time when we were all encouraged to steer clear of one another, stay home, and if we did leave our homes to mask up, wear gloves, and soak ourselves in bleach. Okay, maybe not that last one, but there were days when the world made us think that was necessary.

Were you one who was willing to "risk" your own health for a visit from a family friend or did you prefer the Zoom happy hour from home in your PJs? Either way, no judgment.

It's probably a stretch to say that the modern-day leprosy was COVID, but many acted and believed as if it were true. Leprosy was considered highly contagious, and anyone who suffered from the illness was cast out by the public, shamed, and thought of as unworthy and unclean—except to one man.

My favorite stories about Jesus, as I have mentioned, are the ones that show his one-on-one compassion for someone who was hurting, someone who was an outcast. This is at the very core of Who He is, which is why I am so drawn to it. It shows a level of compassion that could only originate from the God who *created* compassion and love.

We are told, "filled with compassion, Jesus reached out his hand and touched the man" who had leprosy. This man had asked Jesus to heal him and there was zero hesitation. No mask, no social distancing, just compassion.

Sis, this is how Jesus looks at you and me every minute of every day—with compassion and grace. No matter how dirty your soul or your physical body may appear, He has nothing but compassion for those whom He has created. And let me remind you that we are *all* His creations. Yes, even *you*.

Some people want to paint a picture of Jesus with a pointed finger and a furrowed brow, condemning those who have not walked a straight path in life. That's just not who He is. He stands before you, arms open, ready to *love* you. Remember, Jesus did not come to condemn, He came to save.

*My Father, I am good enough for You. Sometimes that's hard for me to remember. I make it about so much more. I try to turn it into something about my worth and value and even my past. In the end, it's always been about Your love. Help me to see it and receive it.*

*Amen.*

# There Are No Orphans

And I will be a father to you, and you shall be sons
and daughters to me, says the Lord Almighty.

**2 CORINTHIANS 6:18**

I grew up in a home with two loving parents. Now, don't
go thinking it was an ideal journey with no problems.
We had the fights, the yelling, the occasional run-away
attempts (yes, I was a little dramatic), the list goes on. Yes,
my parents were loving, but they were not perfect and neither was our home. No home is.

So many of us are carrying sadness and hurt from our
childhood, whether it involves a loving home or an abu-
sive, neglectful one. We all fall short as both children *and*
parents, no matter how you see it. I am sure one day my
own children will have plenty to say about where I fell
short as a mother.

Some of you may not have a family at all. Some of you may have never met your birth parents. Some of you may have been deemed an "orphan." I have good news for all of us today, friend. Not a *one* of us is an orphan. You are a child of the most high God. Even if you have parents who loved you perfectly, their love could never compare to the love that your Heavenly Father has for you. That level of love is *unfathomable* to us. It is unmatched.

Our Father is also one who welcomes home those who have turned against Him. He always welcomes the prodigal home. He doesn't hold grudges and He doesn't do resentment. He only knows love and forgiveness. I know this is too big for our small minds to comprehend—it sounds too good to be true. I feel that, too! But as we have learned, His Word is true and His Word tells us that He "will be a Father to [us] and [we will be his] sons and daughters" (2 Corinthians 6:18).

God is holy and righteous and to be fully holy and fully God means that He is incapable of anything less than perfect. You *are* a daughter. You, sis, are *not* an orphan and never have been. No matter how alone you might have felt in your life, Jesus was and always will be by your side. This is the comfort that a relationship with Him brings. So be reminded today that anything else you have been told is a lie. Satan is the master of lies and he uses them to steal your joy. May you be filled with the Holy Spirit today, which dwells in you now and forever.

*My Father, You love me more than I will ever understand. Oftentimes I don't feel worthy. Help me to receive Your love and grace and enlist the help of Your Holy Spirit today. With You, all things are possible.*

*Amen.*

# *Texting with Jesus*

The steadfast love of the Lord never ceases;
his mercies never come to an end; they are new
every morning; great is your faithfulness.

**LAMENTATIONS 3:22–23**

How many texts do you receive in a given day? Just one? Or maybe a hundred? How many of those make you feel *good*? What if you could get just *one* text from Jesus today? What would you want it to say?

I'll admit that my cursor sat for quite a while as I asked myself that same question. More than anything, I just want to know and feel His closeness. I want Him to reassure me that I am loved. I want to lean back into Him and share the same childlike posture that the youngest disciple, John, had with Him. That's what *I* want. I want my Father to hold me and tell me that it's all going to be okay.

What about you? What do *you* want?

Maybe you need more proof today that He is ___ ___ He is who He says He is. Maybe you need help with your doubts. Maybe you just want to know that you are not alone in whatever it is you are facing. Maybe you just need enough grace and mercy to make it through *this* day.

If that's you, I see you, sis. So does He.

Whatever text you would like to receive from your Creator, you can go ahead and ask. I know this much—whether your ask is written or spoken, or maybe it just comes in the form of a tear-stained pillow, He hears and sees it *all*. How do I know? Because He has told us that He hears and answers *all* prayers (Mark 11:24). He has also kept every promise He has ever made.

Remember, you are talking to the man who predicted the details of His own death, turned water into wine, and made the blind men see. On this side of Heaven, I know it's hard to grasp such miracles and wonders, but friend, His undying love for you is 100 percent real. So whatever it is that you need to hear from Him today, fill in your own blank. He will see it and He will respond according to His will.

Jesus, today I need to hear that . . .

_____

_____

_____

*My Father, we praise You for being the God who never ceases. Thank You for pursuing us, loving us, and coming into the world to save us. Pour out Your mercies onto us today. We know any text we would receive from You would be centered on love, so help us to receive that love today.*

*Amen.*

When You
Understand Who
He Is and Who
You Are Not

# To Understand, We Must First Rewind

Then he said to them, "These are my words that
I spoke to you while I was still with you, that
everything written about me in the Law of Moses
and the Prophets and the Psalms must be fulfilled."

**LUKE 24:44**

I know one thing for certain. God is God and I am not. Neither are you. Sorry to burst your bubble. Because of that, we will never understand all the reasons why things happen, both good and bad. Why does someone win the lottery while another goes hungry? Why is one confined to a wheelchair while another runs marathons? Why is one dying of cancer while another has a clean bill of health? Good questions, fair questions—but still, questions to which we will never know the answer.

Even though we will never understand the plans and the work of God Almighty, you can try to understand why He is always good. My pastor, Hugh Barlett, uttered these words in a sermon and they stuck with me: "In order to have hope for the future, we must look back at the past faithfulness of God." For me, these words provided something I so often crave and want—answers.

While recently studying the book of Job, I was graciously reminded that posing questions to God is welcomed by Him. As long as you're not questioning His character, questions on timing and purpose are encouraged. For you black-and-white thinkers (something I often consider myself to be), the answer to most of my questions is found in one notion—that *everything* must be fulfilled. Jesus told us this specifically about His suffering and death. Every last piece of His story was prophesied. Since the very beginning (Genesis). *How amazing is that?*

So what does this all mean? It means that Jesus is a Promise Keeper. Everything that was predicted about Him *has* come to pass. All but one last thing—that He will return to take us Home. For that, we wait eagerly.

Simply put, whatever God starts, He will finish. Therefore, our confidence must not rest in ourselves, but in God and everything He is. Jesus tells us that we must be ready, because the Lord will come at an hour when we do not expect Him (Matthew 24:42).

*Are you ready for that hour?*

If you need proof today that Jesus is for you and keeps His promises, look back to all the evidence of this in His Word. It all lies within each page of the Bible. Friend, to find hope for tomorrow, you have to know what He has already done and will do. To endure the struggle that you are in right now, you need to know the God to whom you have entrusted it all. Press on, and continue "forgetting what is behind and straining toward what is ahead" (Philippians 3:13).

*My Father, You are an almighty, all-knowing,*
*all-powerful God. Thank you for allowing my questions*
*and understanding how hard it is to believe during*
*a struggle. I know You see me. I know You love me.*
*I want to be ready for the moment You return. Fill*
*my heart with Your truths and Your faithfulness,*
*knowing well that I will one day be with You forever.*

*Amen.*

# I Am Peter

> But when he saw the wind, he was afraid, and
> beginning to sink he cried out, "Lord, save me."

**MATTHEW 14:30**

For years I have thought about taking a risk and stepping out in faith and putting words around my feelings about Jesus. But I was filled with doubt. I still am, if I am being honest. Probably always will be.

My pride and fear get in the way of most things I do and hesitate to do. Can you relate?

Satan, our enemy, holds me back by telling me that others will think I am "holier than thou" and no longer want to be my buddy. I fear friends might see me as preachy or even annoying. I fear that I will sound like I have it "all together," when I assure you, I do not. I fear I lack the theology to write a book about Jesus. Mostly, I doubt that any of it would be used for good.

Let me introduce you to Peter. He was one of the twelve disciples who followed Jesus. He was not the most agreeable of the disciples. One might even question why Jesus recruited him in the first place but, as we have found, the least likely were always Jesus's favorites.

Peter doubted. Often. He was the one who asked how many times he had to forgive somebody (Matthew 18:21). He is the only disciple who left the boat and actually tried to walk on water. He is also the one who denied Jesus three times in order to protect his own life.

Doubt comes in all shapes and sizes. What is your version? Worry and anxiety are my favorites. I am a pro! Controlling every situation? Yes. I am in. Thinking I am powerful enough to fix the problems I have? Yep. Guilty.

I. Am. Peter.

Sorry to tell you, but friend, *you* are also Peter. We all are. We all worry instead of praying, control instead of trust, and talk instead of listen to our Father who loves us so much. We all ask the same question that Satan asked Eve: "Did God really say . . ." (Genesis 3:1).

I did not write this book because I know it all or am the holiest. I am as weak and in need as the next guy. But that's why I need Jesus. So cling to that old rugged cross and pray that we are a little less like Peter and a little more like Jesus today.

*My Father, thank you for loving me the way you loved Peter. Amidst my doubts, my unbelief, my questions, and my denials, there You remain. Help me to remember that my desire should be to please You and You alone. Rid me of pride and fear, Lord. I need You.*

*Amen.*

# You Are Significant, but Not Sovereign

For by him all things were created, in Heaven and on earth, visible and invisible, whether thrones or dominions or rulers or authorities—all things were created through him and for him. And he is before all things, and in him all things hold together.

**COLOSSIANS 1:16–17**

A few years ago, I remember listening to a Proverbs 31 Ministries podcast episode that referenced moms being significant, not sovereign over their children. First of all, let's define sovereignty. Merriam-Webster defines it as "a supreme power." I would say both of those things perfectly describe our God. But! Do they define *you*?

Let's take a little test.

*Are you worried?*

*Is your mind running wild on you? Even keeping you up at night?*

*Are you trying to control situations and those around you?*

How did you answer those questions? I answered yes to all of them. Yikes.

Being sovereign is a lot of work! It's the work of only One—Your Father. You are so incredibly significant to Him, and those who love you, but you lack the control and supremacy of our gracious and sovereign God.

Let me ask you this: How's that going, trying to be all *sovereign*? Tired yet? I sure am. Trying to be supreme renders you exhausted, frustrated, and often leads you to feeling apathetic because it's not part of the plan. Takes one to know one, sis.

Let's hand all of this sovereignty over to Him today. He's got you. He wants to make your burden light again. The question is: will you *let* Him?

Friend, you are absolutely significant. No question. If to nobody else, you are to Him. But let's leave it at that and leave the rest up to the supreme Power of excellence. Let Jesus take the wheel while you climb into the back-seat, where you can watch the road ahead unfold in His perfect timing.

*My Father, You are worthy of all supremacy and
all sovereignty. We laud and adore Your most holy
Name forever in praising You. Help me to put my
pride aside so I no longer feel the need to control and
fix everyone and everything. I want peace back in
my life and I know it can only come from You.*

*Amen.*

# Even Dolly Falls Short

For all have sinned and fall short of the glory
of God, and are justified by his grace as a gift,
through the redemption that is in Christ Jesus.

**ROMANS 3:23–24**

When in your life have you been let down by someone else? Maybe the letdown even rendered you brokenhearted. When others fail us, compromise our trust, or abandon us, it can lead to generalized doubts about the rest of the world. Sometimes that can even leak into our faith life. Has this happened to you?

About ten years ago I was lucky enough to see Dolly Parton in concert. I have always held Dolly in high esteem and consider her to be one of our national treasures, one worthy of a place on Mt. Rushmore. Her concert was everything I expected it to be. Dolly was endearing, charismatic, genuine, and sang all of her greatest hits.

We were sitting fairly close to the stage and as she sang her last song, I turned around to witness the crowd behind me on their feet, arms raised, soaking in every last minute. But I also noticed something else—a scrolling marquee on the front of the balcony that was feeding Dolly every single "off the cuff" word she spoke. No! Not *my* Dolly! It turns out that even Dolly Parton, national treasure, is capable of being the vulnerable "man behind the curtain."

Every last joke, every gaffe, every impromptu remark—they were all planned. Argh. It humanized her immediately and left me feeling a little disappointed with this new reality of Dolly. Now let's be real here—Dolly is and always will be a treasure, and anyone performing on stage every night will need a reminder or two. I can never hold this against her. But it left me feeling a little slighted, as though I was watching a marionette.

Dolly has not been the only one to fall short of my expectations in life. People I love and respect have done the same here and there. What about you? Where in your life have you unveiled the Dolly behind the curtain?

No matter if your story involves a Dolly or a spouse, parent, or dear friend, everyone will eventually fail us in one way or another, falling short of the glory of God. As long as you are putting your full trust in others or relying on others (or things) to bring you peace and joy, you will feel let down; maybe even brokenhearted.

*Friend, you can endure the broken promises of others when you have put all your trust in the promises of God.*

Read that again.

This doesn't mean that a broken heart doesn't hurt. It means that you have a loving Father in your corner when the walls start coming down. He will walk with you, sit with you, and love you through any heartbreak you meet. Even better, He will bring you Home to His Kingdom one day and that is a promise that He will never break.

*My Father, being let down by others has broken my heart. When it happens, I feel alone and trust is shattered. You know this and have seen it. I want to put all of my faith and trust in You. Help me to extend grace to those who have hurt me. Forgive them and lead me back into Your arms. I know that You use all heartache for Your glory. Use mine.*

*Amen.*

# Solitude

And rising very early in the morning, while it
was still dark, he departed and went out to a
desolate place, and there he prayed.

**MARK 1:35**

When is the last time you sat in total solitude?
Or even sat at all?

Certain times of the year bring on a
heightened level of hectic, don't they? It seems like May
and June have become the new Christmastime—packed
schedules and an abundance of activities. While all the
celebrations and events of this season are lovely, my
exhaustion level during this time of year is at its peak.
That's where I am today.

Yesterday I was given the opportunity to sit in complete
solitude: no phone, no distractions, just me, my thoughts,

and the birds chirping. I gotta tell you—it was rough. My mind raced the entire time with my list of to-dos, how much longer I had to sit (the goal was thirty minutes), and then came the guilt for not being able to sit with God in a clear headspace.

Where are you with your opportunities and ability to just sit and be with God?

Often, Jesus retreated to places of solitude to pray before or after a major event. Whenever the disciples could not find Jesus, He usually was in solitude, in prayer with His Father. He knew where to take His worry. He knew where to find His rest.

Friend, we are not built to run like machines. We need rest. More important, we need to rest with Jesus. If you, like me, measure success by productivity, realize that even rest can be productive. It's your time to recharge, prepare for what is to come, and rest in the promises of Jesus. In other words, you are recharging when you are with Him. You are filling your cup so you are able to move on to the next thing in your day.

How might you incorporate this into today? Five minutes outside, no phones, just Jesus? It just might be the most productive part of your day.

*My Father, thank you for making rest part of our routine. Help me to quiet my mind and body when I am feeling out of control. Open my heart and mind to desire You. Only through You can the weary and burdened find rest.*

*Amen.*

# Rich in Spirit

As for the rich in this present age, charge them
not to be haughty, nor set their hopes on the
uncertainty of riches, but on God, who richly
provides us with everything to enjoy.

**1 TIMOTHY 6:17**

I had a pretty big "mom fail" a few years ago that I need to confess. (I have had a *billion* mom fails, but this one stands out right now.) I'm actually a little embarrassed to share it, but as I have said, this is a "come as you are" kind of party, a no-judgment zone, so I am going to lean in.

We live in a middle-to-upper-class suburb of St. Louis. Life is "easy" for most around us, or so it appears. Our area is often referred to as "the bubble," due to the Truman Show-esque sense of protection, cleanliness, and order inside the town walls. My kids, apparently, had not been out of the bubble enough or exposed to neighborhoods that represented the rest of the known world, as I soon learned.

One day, my kids and I ventured into St. Louis to visit my sister. The city streets and neighborhoods are much more decorated and eclectic than our mundane streets. While I thought nothing of the surroundings, I heard a voice from the backseat say, "Mommy, I don't like this village. It's dirty and I want to go back to our village." While my daughter's tiny voice and honesty were endearing, I felt my mama heart sink as I realized the narrow view I had given her in her few short years on this earth.

Even today, ten years later, my kids still need reminding that the richest of souls may inhabit the smallest and most run-down houses. I'm not sure that I have them convinced yet, but as the years pass and unhappiness, divorce, and life hurdles have started to creep into the lives of those around them, it's making more sense.

In the end, kids are kids and kids have a desire for money and *things*. Most adults do too, including me. Over the years, as the kids have suggested that we are "not rich" and that they have a desire for more, I have always answered them with the same response. That we *are* rich—rich in Spirit. To which they always roll their eyes and laugh.

Sis, are you feeling *rich* today? Let me remind you that you are a child of the King of Kings. That makes you the richest gal in town, a princess, nonetheless. Even if your money is dwindling, your car needs repair, or you have just lost your job, your eternal riches remain. You have an inheritance coming your way. The things of this world will only bring you temporary happiness. I assure you of that. They will satisfy you for a bit, but then the feeling fades and you will need more. You may have already experienced this personally if you have a growing bank account.

The joy that comes from knowing and following Jesus will render you the richest in all the land. You are rich in spirit, sweet friend. Bask in all that it is.

*My Father, Your riches are so much more to me than what this world has to offer. Help me to see that. Where You see me drifting toward the ways of this world, pull me back to You. Fill me with Your everlasting Spirit and Word.*

*Amen.*

When You
Think You're
Not Enough

# Fear Is a Liar

Be sober-minded; be watchful.
Your adversary the devil prowls around like
a roaring lion, seeking someone to devour.

**1 PETER 5:8**

The word "fear" and the name Satan are often interchangeable in most Christian circles. The singer-songwriter Zach Williams penned a song called "Fear Is a Liar" and it is with good reason. Satan *is* the father of lies. When Satan tempts us to doubt and fear our Heavenly Father, we are right back where we started in the Garden of Eden; right where he wants us. He aims to break the bonds between God and man and he is skilled at his craft.

Friend, what lies are you being fed today by fear?

Are they the day-to-day lies?

*I'm no good at my job.*

*People are talking bad about me when I'm not around.*

*I'm an awful mom, daughter, wife, friend, etc.*

*If I had a bigger house and more money I'd be happy.*

Are they the lies you have believed your whole life?

*I'm not worthy of love.*

*I don't deserve forgiveness.*

*I'm too broken for Jesus to fix.*

*I will never get over what happened to me.*

Here's a pro-tip. Any thoughts that are not centered on love are *not* coming from Jesus. Nope.

Stop and think about that for a minute. Think about your day and how often those paralyzing thoughts throw you off the path of goodness. I am the first to admit that I am tripping on and off that path all day, every day.

The Bible tells us that "the devil prowls around like a roaring lion looking for someone to devour" (1 Peter 5:8).

But "the God of all grace who called you to his eternal glory in Christ, after you have suffered a little while, will himself restore you and make you strong, firm, and steadfast" (1 Peter 5:10).

Thank goodness, right?

Friend, take heart. Jesus has *won*. He will always win against the schemes of the devil. It doesn't mean it won't be difficult at times, but it does mean we need to fight. How do we do that? On our knees. Take it all to God in prayer.

You keep Satan at arm's length by keeping God and His Word close.

Whatever lies fear is feeding you today about yourself, those around you, or life in general, remember Who wins—the God of Grace. And when He wins, you win. Take every single worry to Him. I promise, He's got you.

*My Father, thank you for being our advocate and protector. You are always speaking the truth in love to us. Help us to speak it to ourselves and to one another always. Where there are fear and lies, help us to fight them with Your Word.*

*Amen.*

# He Made You That Way for a Reason

Now there are varieties of gifts, but the
same Spirit; and there are varieties of service,
but the same Lord; and there are varieties
of activities, but it is the same God
who empowers them all in everyone.

**1 CORINTHIANS 12:4–6**

Before we start here, considering the title of this devotion and the life stage (middle-aged) of the woman writing it, I need to tell you that you do *not* have to go canceling your one o'clock Botox appointment for today. I am not here to lecture you on embracing the aging process or anything of the like. Girl, if Botox is your thing, go for it. I am looking at a bigger picture today, not just one of physical appearance.

What about your *personality* do you wish you could change?

Me? Frankly, I wish I could just chill, be less anxious, talk a little less and a little slower, listen a little more . . . just for starters.

But then I see our reading for today, the chapter on spiritual gifts, and I am reminded that "these gifts are the work of one and the same Spirit, and he gives them to each one, just as he determines" (1 Corinthians 12:11). So maybe, just maybe, He made me a little high-strung, intense, and talkative for a reason. Now, that does not mean I should forget that God also gave me two ears and one mouth. But it does mean that I can pray He will lead me on how I can use these traits for *His* glory.

We all were designed in His image and for His glory. Even if Jesus isn't on your radar and you're still on the fence with what you believe—yes, even you fall into this category. God doesn't make mistakes. I want you to remember that. He knew how He would use you before you were woven together in your mama's belly.

So today, instead of wishing you were different, lean into who you were *designed* to be by your Creator. Pray for guidance and discernment on how to best use the gifts that you have been given. Remember, you are fearfully and wonderfully made, sis. For a reason. Embrace it.

*My Father, You are the Master of all design and I know that I am no exception. Where I doubt myself, fill me with Your Spirit and show me how You want to use me. Open my eyes to Your path and Your plan for me. Instead of listening to the lies of the enemy, help me to rest in Your truths.*

*Amen.*

# That Gray Is a
# Crown of Splendor

Gray hair is a crown of glory;
it is gained in a righteous life.

**PROVERBS 16:31**

A t this stage of my life, the gray hair is creeping in slowly but surely. Now, a disclaimer before we begin today: I am not saying that covering up your grays points to unrighteousness or anything of the sort! Goodness no. If you want to cover up those grays, sis, you do it! You do your thing!

My dear friend Julie often uses her elementary school counselor lingo on me anytime I present her with an obstacle in my path, asking, "What's the opportunity in this problem?" Let's see if we can apply that question to the obstacle that is gray.

What is the opportunity of aging? In the rubble of aches, pains, and hardship, all signs point to a need for a brighter light: Jesus. With each gray, you are one step closer to your Redeemer. Not helping? Too morbid? But friend, *nothing* about Jesus is morbid.

Jesus brings hope, everlasting peace, and a reason to celebrate each day. Every gray hair is a reminder that this world is *not* our home. We are all on a path that is so graciously being paved by our Creator, who is leading us Home. Heaven is your home.

Whether your grays are covered or not, they represent our past and our future. The opportunity is seeing the faithfulness of Jesus in every day, knowing that our grays are a crown of splendor attained by a life of following Him. Is that life always easy? Most often, no. Is that life worth pursuing due to what and Who lies at the end of the road? *Yes.*

You have earned those grays. Every single one. So next time you see one sprout out of the top of your head (or chin—speaking for a friend, of course), smile because you are growing in wisdom and faith as you walk on toward your heavenly Home. Walk on, sweet sister.

*My Father, thank you for so faithfully paving the path behind us and before us. Help us to accept our aging as a means to an end; an end with You. Help us to rejoice in each step.*

*Amen.*

# A Time for Every Season under Heaven

There is a time for everything, and a season for
every activity under the heavens...

**ECCLESIASTES 3:1**

The winds of change are blowing through our house once again. At the beginning and end of every school year, I feel the tugs at this mama's heart—a panic that time is passing all too fast.

My mind starts to wander into the arena of "have I done enough with my kids?" and "what will I do when they leave the nest?" Cue the melancholy music and me thumbing through their baby books.

Whatever the winds of change are bringing into your life right now, you are not alone. No matter where you are,

Jesus remains by your side. He knew there was a time for every matter under Heaven and He knew it would not always be easy. He has been through tough times, which is why He knows your most desperate needs.

Today, as we focus on Ecclesiastes, we are reminded that there is a time for everything and a season for every activity under Heaven. Most important, it all exists under One Mighty Hand. Friend, no matter where you are right now or which direction the winds of change are blowing, One thing remains: Jesus. When the winds pick up, I pray you find yourself gripping on to Him, "for He has made everything beautiful in its time" (Ecclesiastes 3:11).

Hold tight and keep your eyes fixed on the promises of your Creator. He will never forsake you, He will never leave you, no matter how strong those winds might be. Remember, *you* have a purpose and *He* has a plan.

*My Father, I love You for being the anchor You are in the unpredictable changes and storms of life. As we see people, jobs, events, and school years come and go, fill us with Your presence. Help us to surrender all control to You and trust in Your plan.*

*Amen.*

# You're Going the Wrong Way

He will cover you with his pinions,
and under his wings you will find refuge;
his faithfulness is a shield and buckler.

**PSALM 91:4**

I n one of the first deposits into the bank of times-that-I'd-like-to-forget, you'll find the five-year-old me playing with my baby sister, Allison. As our family was putting up the Christmas tree, I eagerly pulled an ornament off and handed it to my little sister, attempting to involve her in the family-bonding Norman Rockwell moments. Somehow, with the quick move of her hand, the hook of the ornament ended up in her lower eyelid. There it hung. There she sat screaming wildly. *There I went.* Out the front door, running into the night. Literally.

In that moment, being the naive child I was, I thought I had possibly ended my baby sister's life, or at least, rendered her blind. I thought what I did was too far gone, so I took off running. It was snowing that night, bitter cold, but that didn't stop me. *Where was I going?* Who knows. I just knew I had to get out of there. Who would want me when I had just murdered my sister? (Yes, I am and forever will be a little dramatic!)

Friend, how often are we like the five-year-old me? How often are we running in the wrong direction, *away* from the true source of help? I should have been running into the arms of my parents at that moment, but the tragic appearance of what had just happened convinced me that they would never want to see me again.

Have you ever felt like you were too far gone for someone?

Have you ever felt like you were too far gone for *Jesus?*

I have said it before and will say it again and again. There is nothing you can do to make Jesus stop loving you. He has called you by name and desires a relationship with you. If you have yet to believe or you have turned away from God during a season of struggle, remember that it is never too late to seek forgiveness and pursue a relationship with the One who created you. He will always want you, no matter what.

Murderers? Yep.

Cheats? Yep.

No-good, dirty rotten scoundrels? Yep.

Come one, come all. He forgives, renews, and showers mercy on you when you need it most. Instead of running in the wrong direction, much like me that night, run to the arms of Jesus. They are open and wide, always welcoming you Home.

> *My Father, forgive me when I have run away from You. Sometimes I feel like I am not good enough for others or You, so I find myself turning to things and people that only render me unfulfilled. Help me to always run into Your arms. Thank you for loving me.*
>
> *Amen.*

# You Are a Work in Progress

Now may the God of peace himself sanctify
you completely, and may your whole spirit
and soul and body be kept blameless at
the coming of our Lord Jesus Christ.

**1 THESSALONIANS 5:23**

What would Jesus do?

This has become an ever-present question, often found on the popular WWJD bracelets accessorizing the wrists of many.

Asking ourselves "what would Jesus do?" is one of the many ways by which we are being sanctified (don't let that word scare you).

Sanctification is the process of being made more Christ-like, more holy. Did you catch that word? Process?

And friend, it is a process that won't end on this side of Heaven. This process takes a lifetime.

Our verse for today states, "May God himself, the God of peace, sanctify you through and through. May your whole spirit, soul, and body be kept blameless at the coming of our Lord Jesus Christ."

So, when will you be sanctified completely? At the coming of our Lord Jesus Christ. Translation: *When you meet Jesus face to face.* Only then will your process be complete.

If you are like me, I need daily reminders that I am a work in progress. The enemy constantly works to pull us off course, but our ever-present Savior's pull is so much stronger. He is walking beside us all day, pulling us back on track, using every bad for good.

Until we meet Jesus, let's extend to one another the grace that we so desperately need—the same grace that He extends to us again and again.

Who can you forgive today? Maybe you need to start with forgiving yourself. Let's ask Jesus to help.

*My Father, thank you for never giving up on me.*
*Thank you for a lifetime of sanctification with*
*You. Stay by my side, help me to extend forgiveness*
*and grace to those who need it, including me.*

*Amen.*

# He Will Never Stop Pursuing You

I tell you that in the same way there will
be more rejoicing in Heaven over one sinner
who repents than over ninety-nine righteous
persons who do not need to repent.

**LUKE 15:7**

Last year one of my dearest friends lost her dad. I had the privilege of walking alongside her the last few months of his life. While it was a highly emotional time, I have always considered a walk through a hardship one of life's most precious gifts when you can do it with those who love and care for you. This walk was no exception.

I never knew my friend's dad well, but John (an alias used to protect her anonymity) was born and raised in the Muslim faith. Those who knew him well adored him, describing him as gentle, kind, loyal, patient, and caring.

The final weeks of John's life were spent in a hospital bed with more uncomfortable moments than restful ones. My friend and her family kept vigil, questioning how many days he would have to endure the discomfort. The days turned into weeks and the struggle only persisted.

My friend, also raised in the Muslim faith, had converted to Christianity prior to her marriage. Her faith is central to her life and she desperately wanted her father to come to know the same Savior who had rescued her years ago.

When John entered the hospital, weeks earlier, a powerful prayer chain began. Mass texts were sent, emails forwarded, calls made, all in the hopes of Jesus running after this "lost," most precious sheep.

John was baptized in his hospital bed twelve hours before taking his last breath. Let this be a reminder that all prayers are heard and answered by God, even if it is not always immediate or visible to the human eye. He never tires of pursuing us, and John was no exception. No matter what your life or religion has been, there is a seat waiting for you at His table. And when you say "yes" to Jesus, *all of Heaven rejoices.*

Friend, no matter where you are or what the timing is, He is there. He never leaves your side and it is simply never too late to say yes. Jesus loves you, He wants you, and He will be there waiting for you to receive Him up until your final breath. Twelve hours before your final breath.

*My Father, thank you for wanting us to be with You. While others may give up on us, You never do. We praise You for receiving us into Your Kingdom, knowing well that it is not what we have done for You, but what You have done for us.*

*Amen.*

When You Say,
"Tell Me More
about Jesus"

# The Alabaster Flask

A woman came up to him with an alabaster flask
of very expensive ointment, and she poured
it on his head as he reclined at the table.

**MATTHEW 26:7**

My grandma absolutely hated wastefulness. If I left food on a plate—wasteful. If I left soda in a cup—wasteful. Being raised with very little, she took it personally if people did not make good use of the gifts they were given. Don't even get me started on how she reacted when I would carelessly wad up wrapping paper and toss it in the trash bag at Christmas! I can still hear her saying, "Don't you throw that away! I can still make good use of that!"

Have you ever heard the Bible story that takes place during Holy Week, where Jesus visited the home of Simon the Leper? I get so excited when I recount this story because there are so many poignant things going on here. First, did you catch who Jesus was visiting? A leper. That's *so* very Jesus, isn't it? He went to visit someone who nobody else wanted to see. Yes, King.

Second, a woman who was in the same house approached Jesus with her alabaster flask containing expensive ointment and anointed His head. The disciples were not fans of this kind gesture. Instead, they were annoyed by someone being so *wasteful* with something that could have been sold and given to the poor. But here is my favorite part—Jesus *reclined* at the table while she anointed his head (Matthew 26:7, emphasis mine).

*Reclined.*

What do you picture when you hear that word? I certainly don't think of someone anticipating their painful death in a matter of days, which is exactly where Jesus was in His Holy Week journey. Instead of being anxious or annoyed or dismissive, Jesus stopped and had this beautiful moment with this woman.

Jesus didn't respond by saying, "no, no, that's not necessary," as we often do when someone goes out of their way for us. He blessed her by reclining and relishing her gift. Oh, how that makes me want to cry. Can't you just picture it? And He told his indignant disciples, "Why do you trouble this woman? For she has done a beautiful thing to me" (Matthew 26:10).

This is the Jesus I so badly want the world to know.

Friend, there is so much to be learned from our King in this story. He allowed Himself to be *in* the moment with this woman, regardless of his anxieties about the imminent future. He accepted her very generous gift instead of brushing her off with a "no thank you" or "I don't have time today." Jesus was intentionally available to her. I encourage you to think about this next time someone wants to share their version of "precious ointment" with you—let them. Let them be blessed by blessing you, and you, sis, will be blessed in return. A little more like Jesus, a little less like us today.

*My Father, Your time is never limited. You are never limited. We see everything through the eyes of this world and forget who You are—a man who was never rushed, never dismissive, and never short on compassion. You see me just like You saw that woman; someone worthy of love. Thank you.*

*Amen.*

# Prayer Unlocks the Doors of Heaven

One of his disciples, whom Jesus loved,
was reclining at the table at Jesus's side . . .

**JOHN 13:23**

I have been asked more than once why we should pray, if God already knows His plan for our life. It's a fair question—one I have also asked myself many times. Jesus loved an inquisitive mind and He welcomed questions, so don't feel bad for being curious about how this all works. Truly.

John was the youngest of the disciples. He is believed to have been somewhere around the age of thirteen when Jesus called him to be part of His ministry team. Can you even imagine why Jesus would have wanted a mind that young in this highly influential group? Well, when was the last time you were in an elementary classroom? There is pure, unfiltered curiosity with no pretense. Children see things with their eyes wide open and I envision John that way.

It is said that John's posture toward Jesus was one of a young child with their loving Father. John often asked the questions that everybody was thinking, but was not willing to ask. Most kings don't encourage or welcome questions about how they run things, but King Jesus met every question with love and understanding.

As Jesus talked with His disciples, John "leaned back on Jesus" (John 13:23). He leaned in a very literal sense. When I hear that, I envision the closest of relationships, relationships where there is ultimate trust and zero fear. Again, what king do you know who imparts zero fear among his followers? Sis, your King wants *that* relationship with you. He wants you to lean back on Him as He embraces you, listening to your every word.

When we pray, it brings us into the same posture that John had with Jesus. A posture of trust, intimacy, and dependency. When you talk to Jesus and share your thoughts and fears, you are having a conversation with your Father and unlocking the doors of Heaven.

Think about it—if you never talk to a friend, the relationship changes over time. It might weaken and eventually the relationship could dissolve. Don't let that happen with your Savior. The prayers don't have to be fancy. The shortest, most effective prayer is often "Lord, help." So lean back into Him and voice every thought and every question you have. He's ready for it.

*My Father, thank you for Your unending devotion and patience with me. I have so many questions and sometimes doubt You. Forgive me. I want to trust You and feel Your loving embrace. Hold me close and never let me go. Pursue me day after day.*

*Amen.*

# He Doesn't Deserve This

Now the chief priests and the whole
council were seeking testimony against Jesus
to put him to death, but they found none.
For many bore false witness against him,
but their testimony did not agree.

**MARK 14:55–56**

The wrongly accused. Have you ever been on the receiving end of this? It doesn't feel good, does it? When I have been accused of saying or doing something that I did not do, it triggers, dare I say, a rage in me. I am a person who rarely lies—I am truthful to a fault on most days, so when I am accused of something, implying that I am lying, I lose it. I pride myself on honesty, so to be accused of anything less infuriates me.

I am sure you can recall a time or two in your life that this has happened to you. Hopefully you demonstrate more self-control in this arena than I do! When we are accused of something we didn't do, it attacks our character. It suggests that we are something or somebody that we are not.

When Jesus was accused of being a blasphemer, His character was questioned, to say the least. He had gone around telling people that He was the Son of God. Now to be real, if I saw a regular dude walking around saying that he was the "Son of God" I would probably think he was bonkers. There, I said it. So let's be a teeny bit fair to those who accused Him. But as we know, He *is* and *was* the Son of God, so He was, indeed, wrongly accused. As we know, He didn't deserve what happened.

When my daughter was little, St. Louis had a big winter snowstorm. Everything was covered in a foot of snow. This happened over Christmastime when all the decorations were displayed in the homes and yards of many, my in-laws included. They own one of the vintage, plastic manger scenes—illuminated and now faded in color after decades of display.

Upon arriving at their house for Christmas, my daughter rushed out of the car and ran to the manger, where the baby Jesus lay covered in snow. In the most tender little voice, she said, "Oh, Mom, He doesn't deserve this," as she wiped the snow off His little body. You are correct, sweet baby girl. He didn't deserve it. He didn't deserve any of it, but yet He took it all on for us. He took on the weight of the world, for you and for me. Because that's who He is . . . a baby in a manger who did not come to condemn, but to save the world from every accusation there ever was made against all of us. He opened the doors to Heaven for every one of His creations who choose to accept Him as their King.

> *My Father, I do not deserve You. But You want*
> *me. Help me to see and appreciate all that You*
> *have done for me, free of guilt and shame.*
> *It is by grace alone that You saved us.*
>
> *Amen.*

# What's Good for the Goose Is Good for the Gander(s)

But the Helper, the Holy Spirit, whom
the Father will send in my name, he will
teach you all things and bring to your
remembrance all that I have said to you.

**JOHN 14:26**

What's the most generous gift you have ever been given? What's the most generous gift you have ever given someone else?

Gifts have a way of making us and others feel special. A gift suggests that someone cares for us and took the time to think of us. It brings out lots of feels.

God the Father gave His Son, Jesus, the most wonderful

gift to accompany Him during His time on earth: the Holy Spirit. God knew He would need it. As a human being, Jesus endured very *real* pain. He experienced sadness, anger, grief, hunger, thirst, and all the other feelings that you and I feel today. Amazing, isn't it? Because He endured all of these very real emotions and feelings, He can empathize with us.

Jesus was able to endure everything He did on this earth because the Spirit of the Lord was with Him. That same Spirit now resides in you and me today. Take a second to take that in. Holy cow.

So how exactly did we get the Spirit in us? Good question. I will try my best to explain. Let's go back to John 14. Jesus was having the Last Supper with His disciples and was comforting them as they panicked over the idea of His crucifixion the following day. So, as the Great Comforter does, He made a promise. He told them, "If you love me, you will obey what I command. And I will ask the Father, and he will give you another Counselor to be with you forever—the Spirit of truth. The world cannot accept him, because it neither sees him nor knows him. But you know him, for *he lives with you and will be in you*" (John 14: 15–17, emphasis mine).

Let's ask it again. How did we get the Spirit in us? Jesus asked His Father to send It to us. Simple and so complex all at once.

Jesus offered further explanation, after receiving questions from His friends. He reminded them that the Holy Spirit "will teach you all things and will remind you of everything I have said to you" (John 14:26).

So the same Spirit that God the Father sent to His Son, Jesus, He has sent to little ol' you. It must be, like, a different variation, right? Like a less important version of the *real* Spirit, right? No! What was good for Jesus is good for *you*, my friend. That is how special God is and how blessed we are. If you ever doubt that you have it in you to uphold the plans of God, rest assured. The Holy Spirit will remind you of everything He has said to you.

How's *that* for a gift?

*My Father, you are the greatest Gift we have ever received. You are the perfect Comforter, always looking out for us. Thank you. Help us to enlist the help of Your Spirit within us daily. Help us to surrender all to You and be led by the One who will remind us of everything You have said.*

*Amen.*

# Every Step, Jesus Is There

And all these, though commended through their
faith, did not receive what was promised, since
God had provided something better for us, that
apart from us they should not be made perfect.

**HEBREWS 11:39–40**

S ome journeys feel long. How are you feeling about
yours today?

If you look at a staircase, the appearance of the
stairs can become a glass-half-empty or half-full scenario,
depending on where you are standing. If you are at the
bottom of the staircase, you see an uphill climb; the glass
appears half empty and your journey may feel daunting.
If you are at the top, however, you see an easy walk back
down; the glass is half full and the climb is behind you.

So, *where are you?* At the bottom or the top of those stairs?

Friend, I assure you this—no matter where you are on your journey, no matter how full or empty your glass is, Jesus is there. He is *never* absent.

There were so many in the Bible who proved this again and again. God's sovereignty and faithfulness revealed itself through countless characters. Consider those in Hebrews 11. This has been referred to as the "Hall of Faith" for good reason.

The passage lists all of those most well known for their utter reliance on God. Noah, Abraham, Moses . . . the list goes on and on. Most of these journeys were terribly long. A lifetime for most. So if your journey feels long today, like each step is rendering you more weak, you are in good company. Those God used the most felt the same way.

Today, be reminded that God has a plan for you. He would never desert you and would never fail you. A good God never fails. He is holding your hand, repeating, "next step, My love, next step."

*My Father, sometimes my journey feels long and even unbearable. Have mercy on me today, Father. Let me know You are here with me. Help me to find solace and rest in knowing that You are carrying me on the days that I am too weak to walk.*

*Amen.*

# God Answers All Prayers

Ask and it will be given to you; seek and you will
find; knock and it will be opened to you.

**MATTHEW 7:7**

G arth Brooks penned the song "Unanswered Prayers" in 1991. In the lyrics he thanks God for the unanswered prayers that have landed him in places that he now appreciates. While the song is lovely, there is no such thing as an unanswered prayer. Sorry, Garth. Simply put, God hears and answers every single prayer spoken through words, thoughts, or a pile of tears on your pillow.

Why do we not receive everything for which we ask? Because there are three answers that seem to exist when it comes to answered prayers—yes, no, and *not yet*. You see, we are *not* promised to receive *everything* for which we ask with a resounding yes. We are promised to be *heard* and *answered,* even when the answer isn't what we want.

My daughter, Sydney, recently attended the Olympic Trials for swimming. It was a week we will never forget. Before she got on the starting block, I asked that God's will be done. That felt like a risky move on my part, given that God's will oftentimes does not line up with my self-serving desires. Truth be told, earlier in the day, I flat-out asked God for Sydney to achieve a personal best and advance to the next round of finals. Heck, He knew what I wanted anyway, so why hold back?

Sydney did not get a personal best and she did not advance to finals. It appeared as though my prayer was not answered but it *was.* It was answered according to God's will, not mine. The answer for that day was no, or at least, not yet. He knew something I didn't and I had to trust that. In the end, Father knows best.

Sis, I know that the prayer I had for that day was about swimming, which seems like small potatoes to those of you who are carrying a much heavier load. If that describes you, I know the answer of no or not yet can feel unbearable. Jesus gets that and He does not like your sadness any more than you do. His ultimate plan is to protect you, love you, and prepare you for an eternity with Him, but that does not make things easier right now as you sit and wait on an answer.

Jesus has told us, "Seek and you will find. Knock and the door will be opened" (Matthew 7:7). Keep talking to the Father who listens and answers. Hold tight to His hand. No matter what the circumstance is for you right now, in the end you will find the doors of Heaven opened for you.

*My Father, You hear and welcome all prayers.
It's so hard for me to sit and wait and to accept
a "no" from You. Help me to trust Your ultimate
plan and keep my eyes fixed on Your promises.
When life gets hard and I want to turn away
from You, help me to turn toward You.*

*Amen.*

# Yours Is the Kingdom of Heaven

Blessed are those who are persecuted
for righteousness' sake, for theirs is the
kingdom of Heaven.

**MATTHEW 5:10**

Have you ever heard of the Beatitudes? It sounds like a midlife beauty ritual, but they are some of the most famous words spoken by Jesus in the Bible. They are some of my all-time favorites, where we are, once again, shown how He took the time to sit and talk with those around Him, making every word count. It's actually all He did during the ministry of His life. He was never rushed, always compassionate and always steadfast.

Matthew 5:1–2 tells us that He saw the crowds, went

up on a mountainside, and sat down. His disciples came to Him and He began to teach.

I love that. He removed all the noise, up on the mountainside, and took the time to *sit*. Every word that describes Jesus is poignant, not to be taken lightly. Sis, He sat. Translation: *He took the time.* Oh, how I need to follow in His steps like this. Do you? He needed His disciples, the future of the Church, to deeply understand how to *truly* follow Him and demonstrate love. What on earth could ever be more important? Today, what could be more important?

Jesus said, blessed are the poor in spirit, those who mourn, the meek, the hungry, the merciful, the pure in heart, the peacemaker, and those who are persecuted (Matthew 5:3–10). Do you fit in there? I love how He starts with those who are lowest on the totem pole, reminding us that to be needy is actually to be in need of Him. And even *that* is a blessing. Where we lack, He is abundant.

Remember today that Jesus is always willing to sit with you and remind you that you are blessed—all because of Him. He knew all too well it would not always feel easy. But friend, according to Jesus, yours is the Kingdom of Heaven, you will be comforted, you will inherit the earth, you will thirst for righteousness, you will be shown mercy, you will see God, you will be called sons of God, and yours is the Kingdom of Heaven (Matthew 5:3–10). It's not a typo that I wrote "yours is the Kingdom of Heaven" twice.

He started and ended His list with this statement. What I quoted here are Jesus's exact words, and we know that He never repeated things for fun. Trust that Jesus only repeated things when He desperately wanted you to believe it.

Sis, yours *is* the Kingdom of Heaven. *Do you believe that?*

*My Father, help me to remember today that I am good enough for Your Kingdom and You want nothing more than for me to be there with You for eternity. Also, help me remember to share this news with everyone around me in a way that is honoring and glorifying to You.*

*Amen.*

# When Your Struggle Becomes Real

# Can We Be Real for Just a Minute?

And taking with him Peter and the two sons
of Zebedee, he began to be sorrowful and
troubled. Then he said to them, "My soul is very
sorrowful, even to death; remain here, and watch
with me." And going a little farther he fell on
his face and prayed, saying, "My Father, if it
be possible, let this cup pass from me;
nevertheless, not as I will but as you will."

**MATTHEW 26:37–39**

This is such a powerful verse. Here you see the actual words of Jesus Christ as He spoke to His disciples before His impending death.

Two noteworthy things are happening here. First, Jesus shares His true and most vulnerable feelings with His *friends*. Then He immediately follows that up with prayer to His *Father*. What a beautiful example of authenticity and faith He has given us.

Does this bring you comfort, seeing that even Jesus Christ Himself felt doubt and worry? Even frustration?

Let's be real for a minute—is it just me or is it sometimes *super* difficult to feel the presence of God and trust in *all* He does? Anyone? Quick show of hands, please.

I see you, friend, with that hand raised. Join me over here on the couch of exhaustion. Today is one of those days for me. I feel like I am spinning my wheels and nothing seems to be going quite right. And it makes me tired.

As a Christian, and someone who likes to write about Jesus, I think I have an opportunity. You, too, have the same opportunity, whether you write or speak or prefer the sit-and-listen route. We can all choose to be *real* and authentic about how we feel with one another, just as Jesus was. But first we're going to have to pack up our pride. Yep. Put it away, sis.

I think there is a common misconception that being a Christian means always feeling, appearing, or acting like you have it all together. Much like Forrest Gump and his box of chocolates, you never know what you're gonna get.

Life can throw you curveballs and, because of that, it's impossible to always have it "all together."

For me, yesterday felt messy, today feels messy, and who knows if tomorrow will be any better. But I know this—when I open up to those who love me and I turn my worry into prayer, Jesus comes running. He is *always* running toward us, ready to meet us right where we are. What makes our journey even more special is, when you choose to reveal *Him* in your storytelling, He will use you for the glory and furthering of His Kingdom.

Satan would have loved for Jesus to just sit in His own turmoil and lament alone that night, because that's where the enemy wants us—feeling like we are the only one going through it and there is nobody to help. If he can just get us there, he will fill our minds with fear and ultimately lies. But Jesus knew how to handle His feelings—He voiced it to His dearest friends and *then* immediately prayed.

Friend, if you are having a day or a month or a year that stinks, don't be afraid to be honest. If you don't have that circle of trust, that's okay. Take it straight to your biggest fan, the God of mercy and love.

So today, let's try being *real* with one another. I'll start.

How are you, Autumn?

Eh, not great. Feeling tired, frustrated, and anxious.

Then let us pray.

*er, today feels hard. I need Your strength*
*nce to get through it. Remind me of Your*
*...ending grace and help me to see the beauty amidst*
*the rubble. When I am struggling, help me to use those*
*moments to reveal Your character and love. Give me*
*the words to share the ways You have seen me through*
*trials and, in turn, encourage others to seek You.*

*Amen.*

# The Lord Is Turning Toward You

Then Jonah prayed to the Lord his God
from the belly of the fish, saying, "I called out
to the Lord, out of my distress, and he
answered me; out of the belly of Sheol
I cried, and you heard my voice."

**JONAH 2:1–2**

The incomparable Brooke Ligertwood wrote a song named "Nineveh" that beautifully encompasses the ever-present battle between the desires of the world and the will of God. The lyrics are absolute perfection and I encourage you to listen if you are able.

You most likely know the story of Jonah and the whale, but do you know how he ended up in the belly? God had told Jonah to go to the city of Nineveh, where stuff was hitting the fan. They were worshipping idols, fighting and being awful. God told Jonah to go preach and turn them back to Him. Jonah pretty much said "no chance" to God's orders. He went in the opposite direction of Nineveh and in turn, the opposite direction of God.

After Jonah set out on his self-direction journey, a storm broke out on the waters. Turns out, God will put you back on His path if you stray too far. In fact, He will put you in the belly of a whale, which is where Jonah landed when he was thrown from the boat.

In the belly of the whale, Jonah reconciled with God. He confessed, "In my distress I called to the Lord, and he answered me. From deep in the realm of the dead I called for help, and you listened to my cry" (Jonah 2:1–2).

Friend, are you in the belly of the whale right now? Have you strayed in a different direction, away from God? You're not alone. It wasn't too late for Jonah and it's not too late for you.

Jonah correctly knew that God would want him to go have compassion on this troubled town of Nineveh, which is exactly why he did not want to follow orders. In the end, Jonah was Jonah and God was God.

The whale spit Jonah out—right on the beach of Nineveh. Only. God.

God gave Jonah the words and he preached to the

people of Nineveh. God showed them mercy and they repented. Why? He is the God of endless mercy—always accepting, always welcoming the prodigal home. If you are in the belly of the whale, God sees you. The Lord is turning to you, just like He did to Nineveh. More than anything, He wants *you* to turn toward *Him*.

*My Father, forgive me where I have turned away from You. Please keep pursuing me and showering me with your mercies. Help me show grace and mercy to those around me. Through you, Lord, it is all possible.*

*Amen.*

# May Your Bible Be Tattered

"For I know the plans I have for you," declares
the Lord, "plans for welfare and not for evil, to
give you a future and a hope."

**JEREMIAH 29:11**

What in your life is worn out from overuse? When you are gone and have moved on to your final Home, what from your life will be tattered?

This question stirred something in me. I talked through it with my daughter this morning. The knee-jerk response for us was these dang phones. The very one I just held in my hand. Argh. I hate the dependency I have to that piece of technology.

I spent the afternoon yesterday with my dear friend Becky, who had just lost her mom, Mary K, days earlier. On the counter next to us sat three worn Bibles, stuffed to the brim with little notes, verses, cards, and keepsakes from a life well lived. They all belonged to Mary K.

As we flipped through the pages, we saw notes she had made, verses she had circled and then circled again. It was a look into her life and what she held dear. It tipped us off to how she leaned on the Lord in her most difficult times.

Pieces of this tugged at my friend Becky's heart, because she realized that her mom struggled with far more things throughout her life than Becky realized. The verses that were circled and underlined pointed us to what those struggles were. What I saw, however, was a woman who, during her most difficult times, knew where to turn. Instead of leaning on an unfavorable vice or burdening those closest to her with irreparable issues, she leaned on Jesus.

Friend, where do you turn when things seem irreparable? Is it working?

My prayer for all of us is that our Bibles be tear-stained, worn, and tattered, while our hearts remain full of restoration, peace, and redemption. Jesus is our only chance at hope and peace. Mary K knew it and chose to live in a way that demonstrated it. Hats off to you, sweet sister.

*My Father, thank you for being our Mighty
Counselor and Refuge when we are broken. We
know you hear every cry, Jesus. Wrap your merciful
arms around us and give us the comfort and mercy
that we so desperately need. Help us to put our
hope and trust in Your Word, now and forever.*

*Amen.*

# Alone

At once the Spirit sent him out into the
wilderness, and he was in the wilderness
forty days, being tempted by Satan. He was with
the wild animals, and the angels attended him.

**MARK 1:12–13**

eing the empath I am, I typically associate the
word "alone" with sadness and pity. To this day,
when I see a woman sitting alone at the movies
or a man eating lunch by himself at a restaurant, it tugs
at my heart. Per usual, my perception of reality is often
skewed and incorrect.

Some folks might tell you that you don't have the right
to ever feel alone as long as you have Jesus, but that just
doesn't feel right to me. I am all for feeling all of the feels, as

feelings are not sinful. Jesus had feelings all the time—anger, sadness, even loneliness. He understands feelings.

We are surrounded by so much white noise in our lives that hearing the calming voice of Jesus becomes more difficult with each passing day. And to understand Jesus and *feel* His peace, we need to spend time with Him—*alone*.

When I think back to some of my most desperate times in life, I was alone. Those times, however, are also what I consider to be the biggest turning points in my life and my faith, because they allowed me to completely and totally rely on Jesus. In those moments, I sat with Jesus, right at His feet. That doesn't mean it wasn't difficult. Those moments *were* lonely, but they were also part of a greater plan.

There are several places in the Bible where Jesus was left all alone. After He was baptized, he was sent into the desert alone for forty days. After an extended period of doing miracles and healings, He went off to a solitary place where He prayed. These examples suggest that being alone is not only *okay*, it is *necessary*.

Jesus used solitude to recharge, rest, reflect, prepare, and pray for what was to come. Every time He was alone, it served a purpose—to rely entirely on His Father. We have much to learn from Jesus, don't we?

If you are feeling alone or even lonely today, I'm sorry that's where you are right now. I am not going to tell you to snap out of it or rise above, because I know those feelings are real. What I will suggest, however, is leaning into the arms of Jesus. If you have the quiet time, use it. Open the door to the One who comforts, talk to Him, deepen that relationship, depend on Him. There, my sweet friend, you will find a peace that passes all understanding.

*My Father, You use every moment. The moments that we often dismiss as boring or lonely are moments that we can lean on You. Help us to find moments of quiet each day and allow us the time to sit with You. We need you, Lord.*

*Amen.*

# When God Is All You Have, You Realize God Is All You Need

Behold, I am the Lord, the God of all flesh.
Is anything too hard for me?

**JEREMIAH 32:27**

H ave you ever been here? In a place of absolute defeat, throwing up your hands in dejection? Maybe you have tried everything and nothing has worked. Maybe that's where you are *right now*. Maybe that's where Jesus is doing His work. *But why?*

I have been there, more than once. In those moments, it was awful, lonely, and yucky. It was also where my testimony was formed. If you are asking yourself what a testimony is, it's the point where something in your life leads you into the arms of Jesus. It has been said that one's greatest "test" often becomes their "testimony" of faith.

My husband and I endured infertility before we were blessed with our two children. Our road involved dozens and dozens of negative pregnancy tests, each one more painful than the last. To this day, whether it be a COVID test or any test involving two pink lines, I am immediately taken back to that very painful place. To say I was brought to a place of submission would possibly be an understatement. I was left no choice but to throw up my hands and fall on my knees. Literally.

I had tried everything and nothing worked. Eventually we were graced, through IVF, with two beautiful children. Praise God. It was here, however, that I realized God was all I *had* and God was all I *needed*. This was something I never would have learned if I had not sat in the dark, so desperately needing to see the Light.

There is nothing bigger than God. Remember that today. If you find yourself on your knees, hands raised in submission, welcome. You are not alone. It's in the darkest, deepest valley where we see the slightest bit of light and walk toward it. If God has brought you here, He can bring you out of here. Hold tight to His hand.

*My Father, You are all I need. I try to make it so much more difficult. I want to fix it all and do it my way. Take my burdens and carry them for me. Help me to see where there is doubt in me and overcome it with Your truths.*

*Amen.*

# Your Faith Has Healed You

And he said to her, "Daughter, your faith
has made you well; go in peace,
and be healed of your disease."

**MARK 5:34**

In the days of Jesus, long-term sickness or physical disability was often thought of as a punishment for sins. How's that for making someone feel good?! Geesh! But this was life before our Savior took on all of our sins. Sadly, there are still many today who live under this failed notion.

As Jesus walked the earth and performed miracles, He was often followed by those who were in desperate need of healing. One story in particular tugs at my heart. A large crowd had been following Jesus on his "tour of miracles." A woman who had been bleeding for years (think of a never-ending menstrual cycle, friend—yikes) came up behind Jesus in the crowd of people and "touched his cloak" (Mark 5:27). She thought, "If I just touch his clothes, I will be healed" (Mark 5:28).

From the touch of His cloak, she experienced an immediate healing.

Jesus felt the power leave His body in that moment and asked who had touched Him. Okay, pause. Let's be real. If I had snuck into a crowd, bleeding everywhere, and grabbed on to a guy's coat and He turned around and said that, I would have braced myself for a lecture for sure. In those days, maybe a stoning! But she was honest and she confessed that it was she who had touched Him.

No lecture, no finger-pointing, no annoyance—Jesus replied by saying, "Daughter, your faith has healed you. Go in peace and be freed from your suffering" (Mark 5:34).

Friend, Jesus wants you to have the very same level of trust today. This woman's faith in Jesus overpowered all earthly reason, yet it was healing. How often do we doubt what could be? We doubt that the doctors have the means to rid us of disease. We doubt that the marriage will be able to survive. We doubt that the behavior will ever change.

Let yourself go there. Let your faith take you to places of childlike trust. I can't promise what the outcome will be, but I can promise that putting your faith into Jesus Christ will never leave you empty-handed. He will use every ounce of faith you give Him.

Today, instead of relying on people or earth
rely on your faith in the One who created it a...
met with compassion and grace always.

> *My Father, You are the Great Physician, the Great
> Healer, the Great Redeemer of all things. Why am I
> so scared to give all of it to You? Strengthen my faith
> and remind me of Your unending compassion and
> grace. You want to help me. Help me to receive it.*
>
> *Amen.*

# When Worry and Waiting Weigh on You

# Cancel Out the Noise

Do not be conformed to this world, but be
transformed by the renewal of your mind, that by
testing you may discern what is the will of God,
what is good and acceptable and perfect.

**ROMANS 12:2**

When my kids were toddlers, I would do anything to prevent them from waking up from a
much-needed nap. For those of you mothers
who protected nap time, you know that you would have
gladly thrown yourself in front of an approaching trash
truck if it meant that your little gremlin could sleep an
extra hour.

The other attempt at keeping their napping cave quiet
was the critical white-noise machine positioned right next
to their little head. That way mama could run the vacuum,

ough, sneeze, or take the time to weep uncontrollably (kidding, not kidding) without waking them.

The white-noise machine blocked out any potential threats to their sleep. Sixteen years later, we still use the white noise in our house when it comes to sleepy time. It continues to block out all potential threats to our rest.

Can you feel it coming? The Jesus transition?

Friend, where do you need Jesus to block out all potential threats to your rest? I could make a list right now and write down about twenty areas where I need it. *What about you?*

When you have Jesus as the center of your life, He can cancel out the necessary noise of this world. Are your eyes fixed all around you at what you don't have, all the ways you fall short, and all the things you aren't? It's so easy for us to focus on all the shortcomings, isn't it.

Sis, let Jesus strip you of all this. Focus on His Word and His Promises. His voice will cancel out all the noise around you if you just lean into it. Doesn't that sound amazing? A life free of noise and trouble?

Just like the sweet babies in their rooms, white noise blaring, you have the option to cancel out anything that is not Jesus. Invite Him into your day. When Jesus is at the wheel, all the things of this world fade into the distance.

*My Father, oh how I want to keep You at the forefront of my life. Everything else seems to cloud my view. Where there is noise, bring calm into my day. Help me to prioritize all things with You first.*

*Amen.*

# If You Fail to Plan

Look at the birds of the air: they neither sow nor reap nor gather into barns, and yet your Heavenly Father feeds them. Are you not of more value than they? And which of you by being anxious can add a single hour to his span of life? And why are you anxious about clothing? Consider the lilies of the field, how they grow: they neither toil nor spin.

**MATTHEW 6:26–28**

When I was growing up, my dad, in his attempt to help me feel control over a situation, always offered one of his most repeated phrases.

"If you fail to plan then you plan to fail."

My sweet dad has always been a planner, and I love that about him. Every vacation had an itinerary that would rival any best-selling travel guide. Every dinner reservation for a special celebration was made weeks in advance. Every day had a checklist and nearly every moment was planned in *advance*. Planning and thinking ahead is my dad's love language. And I love him for it.

Planning and thinking through every possible scenario can take a toll on a person, however. In an attempt for us to feel a sense of control, we render ourselves exhausted and frustrated. We believe it to be the solution, when in fact, it becomes the problem.

What if I told you that Jesus knew this would happen to us?! He knew that worry would overcome us time and time again, which is why He tells us not to worry 365 times in the Bible—one for each day of the year.

In Matthew 6, Jesus gives us two examples of why we should not worry. First, the birds of the air. Birds are void of three activities. They do not "sow or reap or store away in barns" (Matthew 6:26). Let me translate what those three words imply—planning. Birds are not worrying about what tomorrow will bring, so they don't plan for it. And what happens to the birds? Their Heavenly Father feeds them.

The lilies of the field? They don't labor or spin. And they remain dressed in splendor (Matthew 6:28).

While I am not intending to reduce our human existence to that of a bird or a lily, Jesus used these illustrations, so let's roll with it. Jesus only speaks truth, so if He told us to be like the birds, we will do the same.

It turns out, if you fail to plan you may be failing to worry, which falls in line with the will of your Heavenly Father. So take it day by day, sis. Trust that *this* day, God will provide you with enough so you never have to reap, sow, or store.

*My Father, thank you for the 365 times you have told us not to worry. Thank you for the illustrations and the examples and Your most beautiful and perfect Words. Lord, help us to take our life day by day and trust that each day, You will provide. Help us to not get ahead of ourselves, but to focus on the day at hand.*

*Amen.*

# Could We Achieve Contentment?

Not that I am speaking of being in need, for I
have learned in whatever situation I am to
be content. I know how to be brought low,
and I know how to abound. In any and every
circumstance, I have learned the secret of facing
plenty and hunger, abundance and need. I can
do all things through him who strengthens me.

**PHILIPPIANS 4:11–13**

Contentment.

How does that word sit with you? I'll be honest, a piece of me feels a little irritation when I hear it. I know it is something I *should* feel but will never truly achieve on this side of Heaven. In this struggle, I am reminded of my ol' buddy, the apostle Paul.

The book of Philippians was written by Paul while he was imprisoned. He wrote this letter to his friends in Philippi, expressing his gratitude. Bet you didn't see that one coming. Gratitude? In prison? Do you think you'd be writing letters of gratitude if your daily view was from behind bars? I can assure you that I would not. That, my friend, is why this letter of Paul's is so very special.

One of my favorite verses in Philippians is "I can do everything through him who gives me strength" (Philippians 4:13). Many Christians cling to this verse as their sword in the fight of life. Because we will all meet adversity in life. That is one certainty of which we will never escape. Paul knew this and lived this on the daily, all in the name of Jesus.

Let's cling to the hope that we don't have to be strong as long as Jesus is who He is. We have the strength of a thousand armies behind us because He is behind us. That statement alone is at the center of all things content, as it reminds us that, by the strength of Jesus Christ, He is making things okay for you in His time. Hold tight to that promise and that old rugged cross. There is freedom in those splinters, sis.

*My Father, You are all I need. Help me to see that today. Help me to find solace and rest in who You are and all the promises You have made. Where there is discontentment in me, replace it with peace and acceptance. More than anything, replace it with You.*

*Amen.*

# The Invasive Weeds

But while his men were sleeping,
his enemy came and sowed weeds
among the wheat and went away.

**MATTHEW 13:25**

My mom is an avid gardener. Some might say her yard is worthy of an award—a medal for best in show, perhaps. Being the longtime gardener that she is, she will tell you that her constant fight is against the invasive weeds that seek to control and choke out the beauty of her landscape.

Does this ring a bell at all with you? The "choking" of beauty? Are you getting a visual?

I have worked with her a time or two in her garden and

I have witnessed the relentless pursuit of these weeds. In fact, Mom refers to the invasive weeds nearly every time she mentions her garden to me! With that, I am reminded of the relentless pursuit of another, very real enemy in our lives: Satan.

Sweet sister, *what* are your invasive weeds? What takes on a relentless pursuit in stealing the beauty from your life? What is stealing your joy? I'll go first. Pride, impatience, perfectionism, control—the list goes on and on.

What about you?

The enemy we face, however insignificant compared to the Almighty God, is very aware of our weaknesses. Satan and his team of demons have a real foothold on what those weeds are for you. His temptations are continuous . . . and convincing.

A gardener has to work daily on their weeds and so do we. God has provided us with all the tools we need to fight the enemy and all of his temptations. Our verse for today reminds us that Satan is continually sowing seeds of doubt and worry in our minds. We have to be on guard.

So armor up, friend. Equip yourself with the best tools you have: your faith, the Word of God, your salvation, and the peace that passes all understanding. And spoiler alert! In the end, Jesus wins. He will always win. He's the best gardener there is, worthy of all honor and praise and the best in show award always and forever.

*My Father, thank you for being our best tool against the invasive weeds of the enemy. It's a daily battle, Lord. Help us to seek Your love and guidance through it all. No weeds can stand against Your Almighty Hand.*

*Amen.*

# You Can See It Like This. Or That.

Fear not, for I am with you; be not dismayed, for I am your God; I will strengthen you, I will help you, I will uphold you with my righteous hand.

**ISAIAH 41:10**

Have you ever been accused of seeing things through rose-colored glasses? Or have you been accused of the opposite? The cynic, perhaps? I can appreciate either one and most certainly have played both roles.

I have referred to the scary and difficult moments of my life as my "Rolodex of mishaps." Most of our lives involve some level of mishap and mine made up a small percentage of my first thirty years of life. I am sure I have now piqued your interest, so I will share just a few:

—Being trapped in a car with rising water during a flash flood

—Choking and having the Heimlich maneuver performed on me by a teacher on a field trip

—Both of my children choking and having to perform the Heimlich on them

—Watching my child nearly get hit by a car in a crosswalk (wheels screeching) as it came within inches of her

—Sixteen-year-old me running into a kid on his bike and, for a brief moment, he was stuck under the wheel of my car and I thought I had killed him (the child was not injured, by the grace of God)

Those are just a few. As you can see, these are situations where an immediate panic button was hit. These were all acute episodes. Trust me, I have also had episodes that were not so acute, lasting years or longer. Regardless, the Rolodex flips.

Friend, just like most things in life, we have a choice to make. Do we want to see our trials as unfair hands that God has dealt us, with a "why me" approach, or could we choose to see them as reminders that God is always present, protecting us? If you truly understand the character of God, recognizing that He is holy and righteous and always good, then you are choosing to wear those rose-colored glasses with confidence. Seeing life from this angle enables you to see the "God winks" that are all around you every day. He is ever-present, ever-holy, and so, so good.

Let me give you a little more: I am a person who struggles with anxiety in a *very* tangible way. I have all my life. I have been in therapy for twenty—yes, twenty—years to manage it. Now, I could choose to see this personality trait as a hindrance—or I could see it as a trait that has literally saved my life by kicking me into action when life-threatening moments unfolded.

You see that? All those near-death experiences I had in life may have *all* been "winks" from God letting me know that His hand is in it all and He designed me with a little extra anxiety as a mechanism that has kept me on guard for the moments that could have very well ended me.

Maybe that's all extreme and seems silly, far-fetched. But sis, you have the same choice to make. Do you want to see your trials and hardships like this (evidence that God isn't good) or like that (a reminder to stay closer to Him than ever before)? Only you can decide. The amazing thing, however, is this: No matter what you decide, He is *still* there. Winking away, letting you know that it was Him all along. And always will be.

*My Father, Your protection is unmatched. You have saved my life more times than I will ever know. It must be because You have a purpose and a plan for me. Help me to open my eyes to moments of Your grace and mercy, knowing that nothing happens without passing through Your mighty hand. In every one of my hardships, Father, You were there. You never left. Thank you.*

*Amen.*

# Consider the Source of Those Thoughts

We destroy arguments and every lofty opinion
raised against the knowledge of God, and take
every thought captive to obey Christ . . .

**2 CORINTHIANS 10:5**

There is a fine line we toe as Christians. We want to be vigilant and have awareness of the enemy (Satan) while also not giving him too much credit or importance. To not acknowledge him for the true snake he is would suggest he is not real or is not in hot pursuit of our souls, which is unfortunately incorrect. So let's spend just a minute on this today.

Sis, any thought that is not rooted in love and goodness is not coming from Jesus. Period. So stop and think about that: How many of your thoughts during a given day fall from this tree? Often, my thoughts wander into the arenas of jealousy, anger, dislike, doubt, pride, anxiety—the list goes on and on. These are *all* lies and they are being fed to us by a very real enemy who desires to pull us off course.

Today, let's have an awareness of which thoughts stem from a source of Peace and which come from the source of fear and evil. Then we take every negative thought captive! We trap them in a bag and bash it with a hammer. Or something like that. But truly, we cannot keep letting that sneaky snake overtake our days.

Taking every harmful thought captive, as we are instructed to do, has to be a full-on effort. We need to replace every negative thought with a simple reminder of who He is and Whose you are. Try a simple verse from scripture, such as "You have called me by name and I am yours" (Isaiah 43:1). In the presence of God's Word, the enemy has to turn and run. It's just the arrangement.

Let's give it a shot. Not today, Satan!

*My Father, You are over all sources of good and evil in this life. The enemy cannot stand against You. Help us to fight the schemes of the devil with Your word and promises. Where there is darkness, let there be light. Let me be the light.*

*Amen.*

# Forty

Trust in the lord with all your heart, and
do not lean on your own understanding.

**PROVERBS 3:5**

Forty is a number used throughout the Bible to reflect periods of spiritual growth, reflection, and development: forty is a season of "wait." Are you here right now? Are you somewhere feeling lost and possibly forgotten in your forty-day journey?

Oh, how I have been there time and time again. It can feel, in the time of waiting, like Jesus is absent. But my dear friend, He has never been more *present*. Just as those in the Bible who endured a forty-day wait (Moses, Noah, David and Goliath, Ezekiel, Jonah, Jesus Christ), your dawn is coming. Hold fast to that promise.

God used this time of forty as an opportunity for people to strengthen their spiritual muscle of patience. Instead of just giving us what we want, right when we want it, God's plan is usually bigger. If we ask for patience, God will usually give us an *opportunity* to be patient in the form of a trying situation to overcome. Could that be part of your journey?

Instead of trying to determine the reason or resolve for your wait, *surrender*. You will never reach a full understanding of it anyway, for He is God and you are not. Ugh, right? Sometimes, actually *always*, that is the toughest thing for us to grasp. I am with you in your struggle and can absolutely confess that the struggle is *real*.

Instead of trying to figure it all out, just remember that you are never alone. Jesus is standing right beside you, ready to bring those dry bones back to the life He has intended for you. So today, celebrate your "forties," realize that you are not "over the hill," but that you are climbing the hill with a Father who adores you and will never give up on you.

The key verse for today is one of my favorites. It's an easy one to commit to memory. And when your memory fails you, as mine often does, just recite those first four words—Trust in the Lord.

*My Father, waiting on You is one of the hardest things I will ever do. It never seems to get any easier. Help me to persevere during these times and rely on Your presence. As I wait, strengthen me and use my journey to lead others to you.*

*Amen.*

# Jesus Can Take You from Gloom to Bloom

But Hannah answered, "No, my lord, I am a
woman troubled in spirit. I have drunk neither
wine nor strong drink, but I have been
pouring out my soul before the Lord."

**1 SAMUEL 1:15**

Are you in a season of gloom or bloom today? Maybe somewhere in between?

Each year the season of spring brings all things to bloom. But before the bloom, there is a period of darkness underground. Think about the life of a flower. Before it popped its head out of the soil, it sat in darkness. A flower's bloom may appear as though it happened overnight, but what happened in the ground beforehand, in the dark, took time.

The Bible is full of stories of those who endured long seasons of darkness. One of my favorites, one to which I can relate personally, is the story of Hannah in 1 Samuel. Hannah desperately longed for a child but the Lord had "closed her womb." Not only was she infertile, but she was taunted about her inability to conceive by those near to her. This was out of her control, yet those in her circle ridiculed her.

Sis, what in your life feels out of your control right now? We all have something that feels that way, some more painful than others. Do you know what Hannah did during her season of deep sadness? She literally lay on the altar in the temple and "poured out her heart to God." Scripture tells us that Hannah was deeply distressed and prayed to the Lord and wept bitterly. She was in her season of gloom, no doubt.

I adore this about Hannah. She could have taken out her sadness and anger on so many in a plethora of ways. But she didn't. She took her sadness straight to the Lord and held nothing back. She laid it all on the altar. She let out such a guttural "ugly cry" that her husband thought she was drunk. Oh, to show such candid, raw emotion. Hats off to you, Hannah. I bet that felt like a relief, a weight lifted.

I have lived long enough to see that out of the dark comes the dawn. From gloom, Jesus will bring your bloom. When? I don't know, friend. I can't make any promises on timing and I know that is the absolute worst news. But I know this—as you endure life's most difficult trials, God is sitting right there with you. Just like dear Hannah, who eventually did conceive her sweet Samuel, pour out your anguish to the Father who knows and loves you. Climb onto his lap and rest your weary head, dear friend. You will always be met with comfort.

*My Father, during my season of darkness, stay by my side. Instead of taking out my emotions on everyone around me, help me to lay them at Your feet. Extend your mercies on me, dear Father. I want to seek only You for my ultimate comfort and healing.*

*Amen.*

# When You Are
# Weak and
# He Is Strong

## To Know Him
## Is to Love Him

There is none holy like the Lord: for there is none
besides you; there is no rock like our God.

**1 SAMUEL 2:2**

Who is the best person you know? Maybe you need me to qualify that. "Best at what?" you may ask. To which I answer, "yes." Who do you know that is the best at—everything?

Struggling to come up with a name? Same!

My greatest hope in life is that all may come to know the very best person I know: King Jesus. If everyone knew Jesus and everything He is, they would be able to see the depths of the goodness of God. I desperately want the world to experience His goodness. Why do I care? The more this world is filled to the brim with Jesus, the more lovely it will be. Literally. It would be filled to the brim with love and less heartache. Now doesn't that sound nice.

Your God is a holy God, One who only knows the language of grace, mercy, righteousness, and love. Simply put, to know Him *is* to love Him.

Sis, if you truly knew the heart of your Savior, you would know that He can *only* produce love. Anything other than Him is sinful and unholy. Yep, even the person who might have come to mind when I started this devotion. Even you. Even me. That's a tough dose of reality I just gave you.

Jackie Hill Perry said it perfectly: "If God cannot sin, then He can't sin against you."

Read that again. And again.

God is not like us. Thank heavens, right? He is a just God, free of sin, worthy of all adoration and trust. If He is holy, then everything He says is true. If He is holy, His will for us is always perfect. Everything about Him is perfect.

Does this mean life won't be hard? Nope.

Does this mean we won't lose people we love? Nope.

Does it mean all prayers are answered in our own time? Nope.

Then why, oh why would we trust Him? Because He is holy. He is the only One who is, and where there is holiness, there is only good news.

I know I said I wasn't a theologian, but I just threw some

serious "Christianese" at you! And it's a lot. In fact, it is way above our pay grade. Our minds cannot fathom such goodness. But if they could, He would not be God.

Friend, this message of hope is one for the taking. Receive it, believe it, share it.

*My Father, You are holy. You are perfect in every way and even though we cannot truly grasp it, help us with our doubts. More than anything, help us to have blind faith. Put our faith in You ahead of our need for understanding. Fill us with Your presence today, Lord.*

*Amen.*

# What a Friend We Have in Jesus

Greater love has no one than this, that someone
lay down his life for his friends. You are my friends
if you do what I command you.

**JOHN 15:13–14**

Who is your best friend?

That question might prompt a smile in some and sadness in others. A true friend, a very *best* friend, is one of the greatest blessings one can receive in life. But not everyone has found that person. Sis, whether you have found your partner in crime or you feel lost and lonely, I want you to remember something. No friend, not even the best, can do for you what Jesus can.

Why? Because your best friend is human. And just as we found about Dolly, humans will always let us down at one point or another. Jesus is not capable of a letdown. He is 100 percent full of love, compassion, and forgiveness. He will never think He is too cool for you. He will never talk behind your back. He will never break a promise. And friend, He will never forget about you.

On this earth, finding a friend who possesses all of those things is tough. As with anything else, pray that God will bring friendships into your life that refresh your soul and lead you to Him. A friend who is honest with you, even when it's hard to hear. A friend who empathizes with you when you are facing trials. A friend who is *like* Jesus.

I am not sure if and when Jesus will answer your prayer for a best friend. But I know this—He wants nothing more than to fill that void. The question is, will you let Him?

A favorite hymn of mine, "What a Friend We Have in Jesus," reminds us, "Oh what a friend we have in Jesus, all our sins and griefs to bear. What a privilege to carry everything to God in prayer." To me, this is one of the finest hymns ever written. It was a favorite of my late Grandma Betty, who asked that it be played at her funeral. And it was. And it was perfect. Today, let us remember to carry our burdens to the One who wants to bear them.

*My Father, relationships and friendships are important in this life. I know that for some they are blessings and for others they may point to a source of hurt. Jesus, You never fail. You embody every trait of a very best friend. Help me to put my friendship with You ahead of everyone and everything else.*

*Amen.*

# Because God Is Good

Give thanks to the Lord, for he is good; his
steadfast love endures forever.

**PSALM 107:1**

In the Christian community the phrase "God is good"
is frequently used when good things happen to us. But
what about when things don't go our way? Is He still
"good"? Furthermore, is the goodness of God based solely
on our circumstances? Even though I would absolutely
answer no, because that is the *correct* answer, my behavior
often suggests otherwise.

Sis, if we understand the character of God, we will realize that our opinion of Him *should* be based solely on who
He is in scripture and *not* our circumstances. That's a tough
one to swallow, isn't it? Especially when things in our life
are not "good" and are failing to improve. We are tempted

to jump ship, get angry, or turn on our back on God. He gets that, so don't feel ashamed if that is where you find yourself today.

Now, this does not mean that suffering is easy or always feels worthwhile. It means that God is sovereign and our suffering serves a purpose, one which we most likely will never understand on this side of Heaven. We can let our minds wander to places of unfound evidence—or we can base our thoughts on the Truth that our God is *always* good. Most days, relying on that truth may be all we have. If that is you today, leaning on that pillar of strength will give you more certainty than any earthly being or object could give.

> *My Father, You are a good God. Always. Even though*
> *I may not understand the reasons for my struggles, I*
> *trust You. I know Your ways are always better. Instead*
> *of relying on the words of others, help me to rely on*
> *You. Comfort me in my sadness and confusion.*
>
> *Amen.*

# O Come Let Us Adore Him

I will be glad and exult in you;
I will sing praise to your name, O Most High.

**PSALM 9:2**

"O Come Let Us Adore Him." This stanza from the beautiful Christmas hymn "O Come All Ye Faithful" is one of my absolute favorites. It seems to embody the level of adoration and praise of which only a Savior is worthy. While He is worthy, I seem to forget about the level of absolute adoration He deserves. This adoration needs to be robust, and mine is often absent altogether. I go straight into my prayers petitioning for all the things I *need*.

I had the opportunity to visit Yosemite National Park several years ago. My husband and I traveled there without our children to celebrate our twentieth wedding anniversary, and although we had to go over the river and through the woods to get there from good ol' St. Louis, it was well worth it. We wanted to go and see something different, something outside our box, and this fit the bill.

The morning we boarded the bus to head into Yosemite Valley, I was eager to hike and explore. After an hour or so, the bus driver encouraged us to look up and take in the view. We pulled over with the rest of the tour buses and spent some time taking in the magnificence of Yosemite Valley. When I stepped off the bus, I was brought to tears. I was not expecting that! Note that dwindling estrogen levels in midlife have left me with few sentimental tearful opportunities. But this view left me tear-filled—in absolute awe and wonder of the God who had created this view. It was breathtaking. Truly, it reminded me of how the Garden of Eden must have appeared before that apple was eaten.

How often are you walking around in absolute awe and wonder of what God has given you? Why did it take me flying out to California to be moved to tears? Couldn't I feel that same adoration in my home and daily life in St. Louis?

Although we often acknowledge that God's *most* breathtaking views in nature are understood and even expected, adoration and praise for *all* things should be a *daily* part of our worship. It's hard, though, right? We are so focused on the here and now that we go straight into our requests. But do you know what is so very amazing? He *still* listens. Even though we skip over the praise He deserves, He still listens and answers. That's our Father. He's the best. The very best.

Since we all tend to look for acts that will benefit us (you're human, go easy on yourself—we *all* do this), I want you to consider this formula:

Adoration + Praise + Thanksgiving = Gratitude → JOY

Sis, when you come into the day with gratitude, you will find joy. And joy is not based on your circumstances—it's based on peace that passes all understanding, which stems from your relationship with Jesus Christ. You want to feel Joy? Thank God constantly and adore Him for who He is.

Let your morning cup of coffee take your breath away. That first glance into your child's eyes in the morning? Miraculous. Let's try to see things with awe and wonder, the way I saw that tunnel view of Yosemite.

Is He worthy of all this? *He is.*

*My Father, You are worthy of all adoration, praise, laud, and honor. I know this but fail to recount it daily. Help me. Fill my heart and mind with a childlike wonder for Who You are. Everything You have done is for me. Lord, thank you. The words seem too small, but thank you.*

*Amen.*

# It Is Not You Speaking

When they deliver you over, do not be anxious
how you are to speak or what you are to say, for
what you are to say will be given to you in that
hour. For it is not you who speak, but the Spirit
of your Father speaking through you.

**MATTHEW 10:19–20**

In the verse for today, Jesus is telling His disciples about the signs of the end of the age or the end of the world as we know it. Once again, Jesus is foreshadowing what is to come. We know well that Jesus keeps all His promises. Every single word is true.

His disciples were ready-ish to "go" (Matthew 28:10) as Jesus had instructed them. I am sure they were terrified, which is why Jesus was reassuring them of how everything would unfold. These disciples, much like us on any given day, were unsure about how, when, and where to spread the Gospel to those around them. Have you been there? Cat got your tongue?

Jesus prepares His guys for the scenario of rejection with the words "shake the dust off your feet when you leave that home or town" (Matthew 10:14). Someone isn't feeling it? Walk on, "shake it off," as Taylor Swift would say. On to the next town, the next person, the next willing participant. You're not sure what to say? Go back to our verse for today, which tells us that at that time, you will be given what to say. Don't let pride or a lack of information keep you from sharing the good news and love of Jesus. This world is so very desperate for hope. We all need it, and it is at our fingertips if we can just forget about ourselves and rely on the One who reinstates hope on the daily.

Next time you are feeling a tug to speak life to someone, remember the words of your Redeemer. It will not be you speaking, but the Holy Spirit, who lives and dwells in all who have received Him. If you have it in your heart to share Jesus with others, you *will* be given the words and Jesus *will* use you. Put your faith in Him and trust His hand on your back, gently leading you to share hope with the world. And remember the greatest reassurance of it all, "he who stands firm to the end will be saved" (Matthew 10:22). Jesus has got your back, sis.

*My Father, thank you for wanting to use me.*
*I know You are everything I need in order to tell*
*others about Your love, but pride and fear keep me*
*from doing so. Step in where I can't, Jesus. Give*
*me Your words and let all the glory be Yours.*

*Amen.*

# Eye on the Prize

And David said, "The Lord who delivered me from the paw of the lion and from the paw of the bear will deliver me from the hand of this Philistine." And Saul said to David, "Go, and the Lord be with you!"

**1 SAMUEL 17:37**

On a normal day, I like to empathize with my readers. I am an empath through and through, so I love to validate, listen, encourage, and speak the language of feelings. Oh, how I love it. Oh, how my family wishes I didn't love it!

Today, however, I want to work on a different feeling and action. I want to work on perseverance and the fight with *you*!

We are all David, standing before our Goliath, holding only a few stones while the enemy towers over us in full armor. Maybe your Goliath looks different than a literal giant. Maybe it's an illness, a broken relationship, an addiction that consumes you, or even doubts about yourself that creep in daily. Whatever it is, there you stand, with only a stone to throw.

But God . . .

While others doubted David's abilities to fight Goliath, David knew from Where his power would come. He had his eye on the Prize.

Friend, on what, who, or where are your eyes fixed? Is your head down, trying to solve and resolve on your own, or are your eyes on the Prize that is and will forever be Jesus?

David told those who doubted, "the Lord who delivered me from the paw of the lion and the paw of the bear will deliver me from the hand of this Philistine" (1 Samuel 17:37). Sis, if there is a Goliath in your path right now, it is because Jesus knows that you have a David inside you. He put it there. Where you can't, Jesus can and will. Your Goliath might feel too big for you to fight, but it's nothing for Jesus.

*My Father, there are pieces of my life that seem too hard for me to handle right now. I'm scared and You know that. Give me the strength I need today to fight and persevere. Put my feet back on solid ground and establish a deep-rooted trust in You today.*

*Amen.*

# For Thine Is the Kingdom

Yours, O Lord, is the greatness and the power
and the glory and the victory and the majesty,
for all that is in the heavens and in the earth
is yours. Yours is the kingdom, O Lord, and
you are exalted as head above all.

**1 CHRONICLES 29:11**

Awe and reverence. Do you have anyone in your life that you hold at this high level of esteem?

I am a pretty tough sell, myself. I can't really think of anyone. Maybe it's because I hold myself at such a high, often unattainable standard. I also tend to do the same to others. Sorry to you poor souls who know this firsthand! Or maybe it's hard for me to think of someone deserving of this description because there seems to be only *One* who is.

I love the ending of the Protestant version of the Lord's Prayer that reads, "For thine is the Kingdom, the power, and the glory forever and ever." It encompasses the awe and reverence that God deserves and warrants, doesn't it? Friends, I think we are quick to forget that there is only One who *is* worthy. When things go well for me, my knee-jerk reaction is to pat myself on the back. I congratulate myself instead of praising the One who blessed it.

Do you struggle with that too? Without even realizing it, we are implying that we are like God, holding equal power and dominion. This, my friend, is the original sin. That nasty serpent in the Garden of Eden first said it to Adam and Eve when he told them that eating the fruit would "open their eyes and they would be like God" (Genesis 3:5). Being like God is what we want, isn't it? Being like God would mean that we are in control.

Sis, you can give up the fight for control. Release that tight grip. Instead, let's humble ourselves, giving our God the glory He so deserves. For Thine is the Kingdom and the glory and the power—again and again and again.

*My Father, You are over all Heaven and Earth.*
*Praised be Your name. There is no one better. I*
*am at Your feet. Help me to resist the temptation*
*to equate my success with my hard work. All*
*good and perfect things are from You.*

*Amen.*

# When You Love
# Your Neighbor

# Don't Judge a Person by Their . . .

Do not judge, or you too will be judged.
For in the same way you judge others,
you will be judged, and with the measure
you use, it will be measured to you.

**MATTHEW 7:1–2**

nk. Tattoo. No matter how you say it, it's a permanent marking on your body. Most hold an opinion of it, one way or another. Whether it's a tattoo or something else, we all seem to have formed opinions of those around us based on their appearance.

I was raised in a home where tattoos were not encouraged. My parents never trash-talked the proud owner of a tattoo, but there was a general understanding that it just wasn't something that *we* did.

Fast-forward to the midlife version of me. Here I sit with two small, delicate marks of permanent ink on my body. And I absolutely love them. Why? Because they both represent something very special to me. Now I realize, being on the other side of the ink debate, that these permanent marks hold meaning for every single person who owns one. Including me, who once made unfair assumptions about those who donned a tattoo.

Whether it is body art, a skin color, clothing, hair, the way one walks or talks—let's pause and remember *Who* created them. They, too, were created in the very image of God. Sis, let's cast away all judgment. Ask Jesus to give you His eyes so you can see the world in a way that will honor, glorify, and magnify the artist of the greatest tapestry there ever was—a tapestry filled with various threads of different sizes, shapes, and colors.

We all are walking around with a story. Some of our stories might be more physically evident while others are deeply stuffed below the surface. So instead of casting judgment and boxing in folks based on their appearance, let's take on the mindset of the man who sat with *all* who were marked, different, loved, and unloved. I ask you, *what would Jesus do with someone who is different?*

He would listen, love, and see them for who they are to

*Him.* Each is a child of the most mighty King. The work has been done, my sweet friend. You don't have to agree with everyone and everything, but you do have the option to look on with love, understanding, and eternal grace. Someone else does that for you every single day. Let's do it for one another and leave the judgment up to the Father.

> *My Father, forgive me for whenever I have judged others based on their appearance. Help me to see others the way You see them. I want to honor You by honoring those you have created. I don't always have to let my opinion be known and heard. Help me to sit quiet when I should and to speak up when there is a chance to spread Your love.*
>
> *Amen.*

# You Say It Best When You Say Nothing at All

Do you think that I cannot appeal to my
Father, and he will at once send me more
than twelve legions of angels?

**MATTHEW 26:53**

The great singer and songwriter Alison Krauss recorded the song "When You Say Nothing at All" in 1994 and now, thirty years later, here I sit pondering every word. Music is funny like that—it can elicit completely different feelings depending on your season of life. I am pretty sure that back then, I somehow related it to my most recent boyfriend breakup!

Today, the words remind me of how Jesus conducted

Himself. Very few were able to exercise even half the self-control and restraint that Jesus demonstrated throughout his thirty-three years. Jesus often said it best when He said nothing at all.

The most significant example of restraint took place during His death march in Matthew 26. Jesus arrived in Gethsemane after traveling there with His disciples. He planned to spend time alone in prayer in preparation for His arrest. He knew the ultimate plan of His Father was unfolding—His crucifixion and death were near.

As the disciples were plagued with disbelief and worry that Jesus would not save His own life or speak up for Himself, He remained quiet. During the arrest, as His disciples fought to defend Him, Jesus replied by saying, "Do you think I cannot call on my Father, and he will at once put at my disposal more than twelve legions of angels? But how then would the Scriptures be fulfilled that say it must happen this way?" (Matthew 26:53).

Our salvation was dependent on His silence.

Friend, how often do you sit quiet when you have the answer in hand? Maybe your salvation is not dependent on it (thank you, Jesus), but is the relationship?

This is certainly not a strong suit of mine. I typically have my proverbial hand raised, waving it side to side, while yelling out, "Pick me! I know the answer!" Ugh. Isn't that the worst? Especially when the answer has a chance of being wrong! Pride fills our hearts and minds as we try to show how much we know, and that's never helpful for anyone.

Jesus was void of pride. What a beautiful thing. When we choose to speak, we need to remember that we might be robbing Jesus of an opportunity or a moment that He might use for His glory, not our own. In the end, our whole journey is not about what *we* do for Him. It's about what *He* did (and is doing) for *us*.

Let's ask God to help us say it best by saying nothing at all. Our silence might just speak volumes.

*My Father, you are the author of all good and loving ideas. You hold all answers in Your mighty hand. Help us to humble ourselves before You and listen more than we speak. Instead of longing for feelings of importance, help us long for You.*

*Amen.*

# Seventy-seven Times

Then Peter came up and said to him, "Lord, how often will my brother sin against me and I forgive him? As many as seven times?" Jesus said to him, "I do not say to you seven times, but seventy-seven times."

**MATTHEW 18:21–22**

Forgiveness.

It's tough, especially when the sins against you have caused intense pain and anguish.

In Matthew 18, Peter was having one of his heart-to-heart chats with Jesus and asked, "How many times shall I forgive my brother when he sins against me?" Friend, I have news that might be hard to process. Buckle up.

Jesus replied with "not seven times but seventy-seven times." How does that sit with you?

Jesus must have thought we are stronger than we believe ourselves to be, eh? I am sure many of you just bristled at that number seventy-seven. And let's be real, Jesus's seventy-seven probably meant an infinite number of times! Shoot! I'm not sure that I am that nice, that kind, that forgiving. Are you?

Let me answer that for you, if I may. Nope, you're not that kind. But Jesus is. We need Him to help us with this job of "seventy-seven." Remember, where we can't, He can.

All of God's laws and guidance are centered on love. He knows that an unforgiving heart will break you. He knows that harboring hate will eat at your soul and harden your hearts. Friends, when has a hardened heart ever helped anyone?

Everything Jesus instructs is because He *loves* you. He is not asking you to not *feel* hurt, sad, or angry. He experienced feelings and He felt emotions when He lived on this earth. What He wants is for you to *give* your trouble to Him. Seventy-seven times—and then seventy-seven more.

Forgiveness does not mean that what they did to you wasn't wrong. It just means that you have given that heartache to Jesus and, by His grace, you are free. He carried that cross to Calvary for *your* heartache. He's got this.

*My Father, the hurt we carry can feel heavier than we ever imagined. Help us. Instead of harboring hate in our hearts, take it from us. We put it all right at Your feet, Lord. Thank you for loving us through our pain and healing us from our traumas. You make all things new.*

*Amen.*

# Walking Pace

So then, there remains a Sabbath rest
for the people of God . . .

**HEBREWS 4:9**

For you walkers and runners, you know that three miles per hour is a leisurely stroll. If I ever want to get my heart rate elevated, I have to at least crank it up to 3.8 or four on my treadmill. Three miles per hour is a walk to smell the roses, if you will, one where you can embrace your surroundings and visit with those you see along the way.

Three miles per hour is the pace at which Jesus conducted His life and ministry. He was so focused on others that the idea of an elevated heart rate (in the highly desired fat-burning zone) was far from His mind. To be real, oftentimes three miles per hour seems pointless to me. It seems too slow, too casual, and a bore. Anyone else?

Friend, how often do you allow yourself time for interruptions in life? I know I may see someone in the grocery store and duck (sad, but true), not because I don't like them, but because I "don't have the time." Or *do* I? Can you imagine if Jesus was ducking away from the people in His path? What if He didn't have the time for you or me?

How often are we cranking up our pace to four, ten, seventy-five miles per hour so we can accomplish our daily to-dos and elevate the ol' heart rate? While I am not suggesting you ditch your car as your main source of transportation, I think we need to change our *posture* to that of three miles per hour. When we crank up the dial to a faster speed, we might be racing past someone who needs a friend, a hug, or just a smile.

I know the fast pace of life all too well. I am someone who often measures her daily success by productivity. And I will be the first to tell you, all it does is render you exhausted. Heed my warning, sis. Three miles per hour is where it's at—just ask Jesus.

*My Father, help us to slow down. Help us to find our identity in You and Your will instead of racing through life. Forgive us when we have missed the needs that surround us. Open our eyes and remind us of Your pace and purpose, Lord.*

*Amen.*

# Love One Another

We love because he first loved us. If anyone says,
"I love God," and hates his brother, he is a liar;
for he who does not love his brother whom
he has seen cannot love God whom he has not
seen. And this commandment we have from him:
whoever loves God must also love his brother.

**1 JOHN 4:19–21**

What is the most difficult thing you have ever been asked to do in your life?

Your answer might consist of some of life's greatest challenges: fighting a disease, burying a loved one, or overcoming a disability.

For some, their greatest challenge might be one that is often overlooked—loving the unlovable. Does that strike a chord with you?

Oh, friend, this is no minor feat. In fact, I would consider it one of the tallest mountains we may climb in a lifetime. If you are here and exhausted on your climb, it's okay. Jesus sees you.

Today might find you at the end of a rope, where no matter how much you try, nothing works. Hold tight, don't let go. While the enemy is the breaker of relationships, Jesus is the Repairman of them. He is the Healer to every broken heart in the tapestry in life.

The enemy wants you to think that spinning your wheels on your own is the answer. Why? Because it will render you frustrated and ready to give up. Don't let the serpent win. Stand firm against the attempts of the enemy and remember, "We love because He first loved us. . . . And whoever loves God must also love his brother" (1 John 4:19–21).

Love can look like a lot of things. For us, love looked like a bloodied cross in Calvary where God's forgiveness flowed to us. What can love look like today for you? Forgiving the unforgivable? Hugging someone who doesn't deserve it? *Lean in.*

Forgiving someone does not mean that what they did was okay or will be forgotten. It means that the forgiving love of Jesus sets us free from a calloused heart and soul. It means you are relinquishing the justice and the vengeance to your Heavenly Father. He will take it from here.

*My Father, we praise You for being the healer of all things, including relationships. We know we battle an enemy who pursues our pride, but You have overcome. You won and You always will. Help hearts be restored and softened today. Help the unlovable receive hope. Help us to receive You.*

*Amen.*

# Intercede

Some of the most helpless feelings that I have in life typically emerge when I see someone I love who is hurting. They are in the valley looking up and I can't fix the hurt for them. When I carry the weight with them, I often land in the valley right *next* to them. It took me decades to understand how, exactly, to walk alongside someone who is struggling. To be honest, I am very much *still* learning and trying to find the balance of supporting those who are hurting without taking on the responsibility to alleviate the pain. Can you relate?

How often as "helpers" do we feel the need to fix everything for those who are hurting, especially when it comes to our children and family? How often do we over-talk a dilemma only to find ourselves feeling worse or in deeper than where we started? In today's world we look for "help" in a lot of places, don't we? I am just as guilty as the next person for grabbing a self-help book, referring to the words of a well-known podcaster, or repeatedly bending the ear of a dear friend. I am not suggesting those things are awful! But they should not replace the *ultimate* resources of the Great Counselor, our Lord. In the end, His truths will always provide the most perfect direction, even when it seems impossible at the time.

If someone is weighing on your heart and mind right now, pray. I know that might sound trite, but friend, intercessory prayer is the very best way to help someone in need. It's the best gift you can give. Paul illustrated this time and time again in the Bible as he sought to use it as an opportunity to intercede for those who had strayed from God. I know that when I was in my deepest valley, I was too sad and broken to pray for myself, but so many loved ones interceded religiously for me. For that, I am eternally grateful.

Intercession leads to unity. In a word so severely divided, we need more opportunity to intercede and be reminded that we are all members of the same family. No matter who you are or what you believe, we were created by the same God. Let that be our starting point.

Whoever is on your mind today, pray for them right now. Ask God that they be strengthened and filled with His goodness today so they may know His abundant love. And, if it is you who needs the intercessory prayer and prayer seems too hard today, that's okay. God will meet you there. But remember, God can't take away what you won't give Him. Lean into His love today. Trust Him with whatever it is that has got a hold on you. We *all* need prayer and we *all* need Jesus.

*My Father, thank you for being the Greatest Counselor I could ever have. Sometimes, because I cannot see You, it is hard to talk to You and pray, believing that it will help. I look for help in other places and forget about the Words You have given me. Lord, instead of us trying to fix each other, remind us to bring it all to You in prayer. Our greatest chance for healing is through You and You alone.*

*Amen.*

# When You Surrender and Go

# It's Not about You

And we know that for those who love God
all things work together for good, for those
who are called according to his purpose.

**ROMANS 8:28**

The first line of the best-selling book *The Purpose Driven Life* by Rick Warren reads, "It's not about you."

Readers pick up this book in the hope of trying to uncover a deeper meaning and purpose in their lives. When they open it, they are met face-to-face with this very humbling statement.

What feelings does that statement elicit in you?

My first reaction is probably a dirty look, to be honest. Nobody likes hearing that something is not about them! If you are like me, however, the first reaction is often the wrong reaction. My first reaction is always a very human, prideful reaction.

If you stop and think about it, though, that statement takes all the pressure off us. If everything we do and say and buy and lean into is not about us, then who, might you ask, is it about?

Jesus.

It all goes back to surrender. Once you realize that this whole life of yours is not about you, but about Jesus, your entire perspective of life will change. That doesn't mean that you will no longer strive for the attention of this world or erase sin from your life; it means that your posture in life changes from one of "all about me" to "all about Him." Easy? Nope. Worth it? Yes.

We have all been called according to His purpose. Friend, you can stop searching for purpose for your life. You can stop spinning your wheels trying to uncover hidden meaning, picking up every self-help book promising to uncover the "real" you. Living for Jesus, telling others about Him, and spending time with Him—here we will find our purpose.

"Many are the plans in a man's heart, but it is the Lord's purpose that prevails" (Proverbs 19:21).

*My Father, help us to make everything we do be for You and about You. Strip us from our selfish desires and our deepest insecurities. Help us to stop searching for answers when You, Lord, are the Answer. Today, help us to see and know that all roads point to You.*

*Amen.*

# Follow Me

Then Jesus told his disciples, "If anyone would come after me, let him deny himself and take up his cross and follow me. For whoever would save his life will lose it, but whoever loses his life for my sake will find it."

**MATTHEW 16:24–25**

Many of you may have watched *The Chosen*, a multi-season series about the life of Jesus. While there are different schools of thought surrounding the show, I love it for revealing the gentleness and kindness of Jesus in a very real, tangible way. I have been moved to tears numerous times because Jesus is so accurately portrayed as the beloved friend He is. He wipes the tears of sinners, washes the feet of the unclean, and surrounds Himself with the meek and unworthy.

Do you fit into any of those categories? I sure do.

Jesus's disciples fit every one of those categories. Don't you just love that about our Savior? He picks the least of us and says "yes." As He encountered each disciple along His journey, He prompted them with the same words: "follow me." It was ever-so-gentle and instructional, yet *optional*. I love that God's grace renews our will and opens our hearts to see how good and *necessary* it is to trust in Jesus. Remember that even more astounding than our *choice* to follow Him is the infinite grace that God has gifted us. Grace upon grace upon grace.

To follow Him is what He is asking each of us to do, and just like the disciples, we are being given the choice. He *wants* you to choose Him, but he gives you the free will to do it.

Does following Him feel like too much of a commitment? Too overwhelming? If your answer is yes, you are correct. Jesus knew it would not be easy, which is why He sent His Holy Spirit to intercede and help. Remember, you are not alone, sis. You never are.

If you are ready to follow Him, tell Him. Don't waste another minute. Pray this prayer with me.

*My Father, I know I'm a sinner and I ask for Your forgiveness. I believe Jesus Christ is Your Son. I believe that He died for my sins and that You raised Him to life. I want to trust Him as my Savior and follow Him as Lord from this day forward. Guide my life and help me to do your will. I pray this in the name of Jesus.*

*Amen.*

# This, Then, Is How You Pray

And when you pray, do not keep on babbling like
pagans, for they think they will be heard because
of their many words. Do not be like them, for your
Father knows what you need before you ask him.

**MATTHEW 6:7–8**

Have you ever been asked to pray out loud, in front
of people? How did you feel about that?

If you had asked me that question several years
ago, I would have told you that I don't feel good enough,
eloquent enough, qualified enough, or calm enough to
carry it out. It *terrified* me. Can you relate?

I have heard it said that the biggest thing standing in
the way of our prayer life is pride. Pride can look like a lot of
things. It can look like thinking you know more than God.
It can look like worry over sounding silly and unqualified

to those around you. Turns out, all my fears around prayer were (and are) 100 percent based on pride. Argh!

Prayer can quickly become a time to flaunt your extended vocabulary, your theology knowledge, or your public speaking abilities. But *none* of that matters to God. He just wants your heart. He could care less about all the frills that we deem important.

Let's refer to what Jesus himself said about prayer. He often did it quietly and alone. In addition to encouraging solitude during prayer time, He also gifted us with the words through the Lord's Prayer. Why have we tried to recreate something that was already so perfectly created? The work has already been done.

Friend, when all else fails, pray like this. When you are not sure where to start, pray like this. When you are too nervous to come up with the words on your own, pray like this. When all you have left are tears, pray just like this:

*Our Father in Heaven, hallowed be Your name, Your kingdom come, Your will be done, on earth as it is in Heaven. Give us today our daily bread. Forgive us our debts, as we also have forgiven our debtors. And lead us not into temptation, but deliver us from the evil one.*

It was His prayer. Let it also be yours.

# Go

Now the eleven disciples went to Galilee, to the mountain to which Jesus had directed them. And when they saw him they worshiped him, but some doubted. And Jesus said to them, "All authority in Heaven and on earth has been given to me. Go therefore and make disciples of all nations, baptizing them in the name of the Father and of the Son and of the Holy Spirit, teaching them to observe all that I have commanded you. And behind, I am with you always, to the end of the age."

**MATTHEW 28:16–20**

These are the last words spoken to the disciples before Jesus ascended into Heaven following His death and resurrection. These words are referred to as "the great commission." It is what all Christians have been called to do. Intimidating, right?! Me? Make disciples of all nations? What?

Friend, if you are doubtful, like His friends were, that's okay. As you just read, some worshiped, some doubted. That's still the case today. Even the most devout Christians doubt, including me. Doubting and questioning God is what led to the original sin of Eve eating a forbidden apple. With that, we come by doubt and questioning honestly. It's in our bones. God even *expects* it.

Even if you doubt, you are still welcome here. Jesus hears your doubts and He still wants you.

The most reassuring piece of this verse for me is the reminder of *when* He is with you and me. *Always.* He is *always* with us. Until the end of the ages.

*My Father, thank you for loving me unconditionally. Thank you for accepting me, doubts and all. I humble myself at Your feet, asking for You to lead me and help me with my unbelief. Help me to feel your peace as I am reminded that You, Lord, are always with me.*

*Amen.*

# Let Down Your Nets

And when he had finished speaking,
he said to Simon Peter, "Put out into the deep
and let down your nets for a catch."

**LUKE 5:4**

My husband and son share a love of fishing. They live for quiet summer nights at the lake behind our house where they can sit in solitude, casting their lines over and over, sometimes pulling in a picture-worthy bass and sometimes coming home empty-handed. Fishing is tricky—it involves a complete lack of control over what lies beneath the water. Giving up the control is hard, as it often leads to long stretches of waiting and, more often than not, disappointment. But oh man . . . when you hook that fish, the moment is worth the wait.

Jesus's disciples knew this all too well. Luke 5 takes us to the disciples in their boats, exhausted and empty-handed after days of fishing with no result. Their nets came up empty again and again and they were famished. Enter Jesus. He calmly says to Peter, "put out into deep water, and let down the nets for a catch" (Luke 5:4).

Jesus telling them to let down their nets feels a little patronizing in the moment, given their recent run of bad luck. Why would they be stupid enough to go back out on the water and continue their futile pursuit? It made *zero* sense and you can bet that our honest-to-a-fault brother, Peter, let Jesus know. Peter told Jesus they had been up all night to no avail, but he quickly conceded, saying, "because you say so, I will let down the nets." *Good boy, Peter.*

Is Jesus asking you to let down your nets and trust Him in an area of your life that seems hopeless? Do you feel broken, tired, emotionally famished, and struggling to let down your nets in the fear that they will surface empty—yet again?

Just like Jesus understood the eye rolls of His disciples, He also understands your hesitation. Much of what Jesus said and did seemed unbelievable and hard to grasp, yes, but that is why He is God and we are not. If you feel like the disciples, hesitant to believe and trust, ask God for what you need, sis. I promise you that He is the only *real* hope we have. I can't promise that your nets will come up full, but I know that leaning on Jesus *never* leaves you feeling empty.

On that day, Peter and the disciples' nets finally surfaced *so* full of fish that they had to call for backup. What was once empty was now overflowing.

*My Father, some days it's harder to trust You than*
*I like to admit. Forgive my doubt and disbelief.*
*Give me the faith I need to rely on You always.*
*Remind me that Your Holy Spirit lives within me.*
*I don't have to be strong when You are. Jesus, help*
*me to trust You this very day and walk with You.*

*Amen.*

# The Laws of Love

I am the Lord your God, who brought you out of
the land of Egypt, out of the house of slavery.

**EXODUS 20:2**

How many of the Ten Commandments could you recite by memory?

If you can't recite any, I understand. It's a lot to remember. The commandments also carry a fair amount of guilt with them, don't they? I think some people purposefully avoid knowing them, while some have never been exposed, while others are told they are not "good enough" to be a Christian if they don't uphold every single one of them. I have good news today—I understand all those responses and so does Jesus. I hope that after reading this, you will understand the *why* behind the Law of God.

Let me ask you this: As a child, did you have a fair amount of boundaries put into place by your parents? I would assume that whoever raised you gave you some form of discipline and structure for how to live and how to survive. Yes? *Why did they do that?* To protect you from the harm that comes from not adhering to the rules of life.

A loving father would do just that, wouldn't he? Sis, the laws that God put into place were to *protect* you and me. They are *all* laws of love. Because God loves us so intensely, He gave us a list of to-dos that we should follow in order to avoid the pains and anguish of life. He knew that breaking the commandments would have earthly consequences, and regardless of your role, victim or assailant, it would cause emotional pain.

To understand the commandments, we have to reflect on the holy nature of God. A holy, righteous God is *only* capable of love—He never varies from it or compromises it. If He gave us these laws, the underlying reason is and always will be because of His infinite love for us.

The world has tried to overcomplicate this and paint a picture of an angry God who looks to condemn. Jesus took all of our condemnation on when He died on the cross. The Ten Commandments should absolutely be followed, but when we stumble, we are still saved by grace alone if we believe that Jesus is who He says He is.

Your ticket into Heaven has already been purchased with the blood of Jesus. Period. Your inability to keep the commandments does not render you a failure; it renders you in need of a Savior. Friend, we are *all* in need of a Savior. So if you want these laws to lead you to the path of righteousness, then stay close to the One who paved it. Everything that God allows is for His glory and to draw His people closer to Him. These commandments are no exception.

**And just in case you want the full list, here you go:**

1. Have no other gods before me
2. Do not make idols
3. Do not take God's name in vain
4. Keep the Sabbath holy
5. Honor your father and mother
6. Do not murder
7. Do not commit adultery
8. Do not steal
9. Do not make up lies about others
10. Do not want what others have

*My Father, You are merciful and loving at all times. All Your ways are holy. Thank you for these laws of love. Help us to abide by them and keep You first in all things we do. We cannot keep these laws without remaining close to You. Draw us near today.*

*Amen.*

# All for His Glory

So, whether you eat or drink, or whatever
you do, do all to the glory of God.

**1 CORINTHIANS 10:31**

When I quit work to become a stay-at-home mom sixteen years ago, my job title changed. I went from being an Academic Training Leader at a Fortune 500 company to just Mom. Have you had a title change in life? My guess is that you've probably been through more than one. How did your title change? Did it change how you felt about yourself?

I remember when I was first asked "what do you do" by someone after I decided to stay home. My response, apologetically, was "I'm just a stay-at-home mom." Even typing that makes me want to cry because it was my forever dream. A dream I never thought I would have, yet here I was, feeling a sense of shame about it, like it was not enough. How many times in life do we do that to God? We ask for a prayer to be answered, only to find that it is *still* not enough for us.

Isn't that feeling of "not enough" just the worst?! I struggle with it more often than I would like to admit. Anyone is capable of feeling this at any time—it could be in regard to a job title, a relationship, a living arrangement, your social schedule, et cetera. All of this can make us feel like we are not enough. And sis, it's *all* a lie. God can use anything and anyone for His glory and I assure you, He wants to use *you* no matter what your role in life is.

I don't care if you are "just" a mom, wife, janitor, scientist, CEO, professional athlete, receptionist, or teacher. Every role can be used to glorify God no matter how mundane, routine, or insignificant it might feel. There is an opportunity to serve others, offer grace and kindness to all of God's children each and every day if you just— look. Answering phones? Do it with a smile. Presenting to a room full of people? Do it with humility. Teaching a classroom of kids? Love them like Jesus. Scrubbing floors? Praise God for the physical ability to work.

All for His glory, girl. All of it. You are significant and enough, no matter what your role is. Your "job" or line of work is not a reflection of your worth. Your standing as a child of the One True King is your worth. Your opportunity to serve Him is your worth. And there is no greater identity or job title than that.

*My Father, You created me for a purpose. Your purpose. I have tried to make this whole thing about me when this whole thing is about You. Forgive me and lead me to see every day as a way to glorify You and Your Kingdom.*

*Amen.*

# Go—Tell Your Story

Go therefore and make disciples of all nations,
baptizing them in the name of the Father and of
the Son and of the Holy Spirit, teaching them to
observe all that I have commanded you.

**MATTHEW 28:19–20**

Recently I conducted a survey asking what was holding people back from sharing the good news about Jesus with others. Two answers stood out from the rest. First, a lack of knowledge, both about Jesus and about how to weave Him into the conversation. Second, a fear of coming off as "holier than thou" to their audience of friends and family. Can you relate? I sure can, as I worry about the exact same things. It's part of why I was so anxious about writing this devotional. As I told you before, I am not a theologian or an esteemed author. I am a sinner at the very core and I had so many thoughts holding me back from starting this project.

But sis, I can tell you right now that you are the perfect one for the job of spreading the good news of Jesus. I am 100 percent certain of it.

How do I know? Well, because you are sitting there with breath in your lungs. That alone tells me that you have a story to share. We all do.

Did you know that Jesus did all of His teaching (not preaching) through the telling of stories? "With many similar parables Jesus spoke the word to them, as much as they could understand. He did not say anything to them without using a parable" (Matthew 4:33–34). Did you hear that? He didn't point His finger or make demands when He spoke. But every story demonstrated our need for a Heavenly Father who loves, forgives, accepts, and redeems. Where there is a need, there is an opportunity to *go* and spread the love of Jesus.

So what story could you share? The one that is unapologetically *yours*. It doesn't have to be pretty or perfect. In fact, the more tattered and torn your tapestry is, the more approachable you become and the more reputable your story. Struggle is our great equalizer. We all have a bucket of issues, so let's use them for good. What the devil meant for bad, God *always* meant for good. The good of His Kingdom that has *no* end.

When we share our struggles, walls come down, bonds are formed, and relationships are deepened. Jesus will meet you right where you are and He will do the same for your audience. My greatest opportunities to talk about the love of Jesus have always stemmed from a difficult time in my life or in the lives of those around me. If we aren't going to see one another through those times, leading one another into the arms of Jesus, then friend, what on earth are we doing here? Truly. What is this all for if it's not to be loved by Jesus and give love to one another?

So go on, tell your story. Be brave enough to plant the seed and He will take it from there . . .

*My Father, humble me with Your presence. Use me today to further Your Kingdom. Soften my heart and the hearts of those around me. Start a revival in this world that cannot be denied. A revival that reminds us that we are all loved, invited, and heirs to an eternal inheritance.*

*Amen.*

# *Acknowledgments*

I quite frankly, cannot comprehend that this all happened—that I wrote this book in a matter of months. But when I look at my circle of support, it all makes sense to me.

I am eternally grateful to my husband, Andy, for his belief in me. We knew that writing and publishing this book was a risk and Andy's response to that was "if I ever had to take a risk on anything or anyone, it would be you." They were the kindest, most genuine words anyone has ever said to me. Andy, Jesus knew what He was doing when He gave you to me. Without you I am only half a person. You in my life enables me to be who God fully intended me to be. I love you so much.

To my sweet babies, Sydney and Ben, thanks for letting Mom sit in her office, for sometimes hours on end, as you entertained yourselves. I hope you know why I wrote this book—always remember why we are all here. And remember that, way before this book, you two were my first, most amazing creations. I am prouder of you than you'll ever know.

To Mom and Dad, thank you for believing that *everything* I do is amazing. You convinced me, a girl with mediocre talents, that I could do anything—and then convinced me that it was perfect. Your love, encouragement, and pride in me have given me confidence and comfort. I love you both so much.

A very special thanks to Hugh and Judy Barlett for helping to ensure that this project was honorable to the Father who created me. I asked you to read this in record time, knowing your time is limited, and you did it. I value your input so very much and have great admiration for you both.

To my original editor, Liza Cooper, you are amazing. You, too, edited this book in record time, leading Greenleaf Publishing to say it was in the "top 10 percent of their cleanest submissions." Wow. Thank you for being you and for being so readily available to help me—I am forever grateful.

To those at Greenleaf Book Group, thank you for taking a risk on this newbie and making it so easy. I am still and forever will be in disbelief that someone picked me to write a book. You made me a published author—thank you.

To Betty Wilke, you would tell me that you're not fancy enough to be part of a book, but you were right there with me the entire time. I remember every hug, every prayer, every ride to Sunday School, and watching you love everyone around you. I remember the loving hand squeeze that you gave every person we passed in the nursing home halls. I remember seeing all the people in need who came through your house because they knew their needs would be met with you. I remember that you found all your strength in one man, Jesus Christ. You, Grandma, are as fancy as it gets. Fancy and adored by everyone who knew you.

To Jesus, You are my beacon of hope, the only light that has never gone out in my life. Thank you for the unending goodness that you bring out of every high and every low of my journey. I pray that I have made You proud with this book, that I am the good and faithful servant You designed me to be. It was *all* for You. I know I mess up all the time, but my heart is *with* you. Always. And I dream of the day we meet so I can stand in awe, speechless, knowing that only through You did I do *that*. That life that I gave to You. Forever I will bask in your goodness, my King.

# About the Author

 **AUTUMN SCHOECK** is a regular lady who wrote a book. Fueled by her love of Jesus and a deep desire for unashamed authenticity (think messed-up hair and sweatpants), Autumn invites her readers into a place where chaos meets comfort and worry meets Jesus. She lives in St. Louis, Missouri, with her husband and two children, where she is constantly trying exercise but never seems to have the time. *This Feels Like Home* is Autumn's debut devotional.

Made in the USA
Las Vegas, NV
17 May 2025

22330296R00142